About this Publication

Title:
Multi-crew Co-operation

Series:
For Helicopter Pilots

Edition:
First published 2018, Second Edition, May 2022

Principal Author:
Mike Becker, ATPL(H), FIR, FER, Diploma (Training and Assessment)

Editor:
Bev Austen, BTech(CompSt), MEd(DTL)

Copyright
Copyright © 2022 Becker Helicopter Services Pty Ltd

Photos and Illustrations

Most photos and illustrations in this document have been sourced from Becker Helicopter Services Pty Ltd. The remainder is taken from the internet from various sources; Every effort has been made to ensure images with public domain or Creative Commons Licences have been used and/or appropriate attribution provided.

Disclaimer

Nothing in this text supersedes any operational documents issued by any civil aviation authority or regulatory body, aircraft, engine, and avionics manufacturers or the operators of aircraft throughout the world. No responsibility is taken for the interpretation and application of the information contained in this document. Managing the safety of the aircraft is the sole responsibility of the pilot-in-command.

Every possible effort has been made to establish the accuracy of the information contained in this book; however, the author, Becker Helicopter Services Pty Ltd, accept no responsibility for errors or omissions.

The Publisher and the Author make no representations or warranties for the accuracy or completeness of the contents of this work and expressly disclaim all warranties, including without limitation warranties of fitness for a particular purpose. No warranty may be created or extended by sales or promotional materials. The advice and strategies contained herein may not be suitable for every situation. This work is sold with the understanding that the author is not engaged in rendering legal, accounting, or other professional services. If professional assistance is required, the services of a competent professional person should be sought. Neither the Publisher nor the Author shall be liable for damages arising therefrom.

The fact that an organisation or website is referred to in this work as a citation and/or a potential source of further information does not mean that the author or the publisher endorses the information the organisation or website may provide or recommendations it may make. Further, readers should be aware that internet websites listed in this work may have changed or disappeared between when this work was written and when it is read.

Contents

About this Publication 1
Contents 2
About this Book 5
About the Author 6

Introduction 7

Risk Management 10
Key Definitions 11
Identifying Hazards 12
Risk Assessment (Analysis) 13
Controlling the Risk: Risk Mitigation 15

Threat Error Management 17
TEM Principles and Model 17
Threats and Threat Management 19
    External Threats 19
    Internal Threats 21
    Threat Management 21
Errors and Error Management 22
    Error Management 23
Undesired Aircraft State 24
Application of TEM 25
Countermeasures 26
Summary 28

Crew Resource Management 29
Objectives of CRM 30
Establish and Maintain Team Relationships 30
    Aircrews are Teams 30
    Cockpit Gradient 31
    Ego States 34
Verbal Communication 36
    Active Listening 38
    Stress and Conflict 38
    Team Communication 40
    1. Communicate in the Same Language 41
    2. Communicate Positively 41
    3. Communicate Accurately 41
    4. Direct Assistance 43
    5. Announce Actions 44
    6. Offer Assistance 44
    7. Acknowledge Actions 44
    8. Be Explicit 44
    9. Provide Aircraft Control and Obstacle Advisories 45
    10. Co-ordinate Action Sequence and Timing 45
    Practice Good Intercom Discipline 45
Conduct Mission Planning and Rehearsal 46
Establish and Maintain Appropriate Workloads 47
Exchange Mission (Sortie/Task) Information 48
Cross Monitor Performance 49
CRM for the Single Pilot 50

- Decision-Making Techniques 51
  - 3Ps Model 53
  - DECIDE Model 53
  - GRADE Model 53
  - Analytical decision making 54
  - Get-There-itis 54
  - Attitude 55
  - Operational Pitfalls 56
- Phraseology 57
- Case Study 61
- Summary 61

Multi-Crew Cooperation (MCC) 62

- MCC Core Principles 62
- Shared Responsibilities 66
- Crew Positions 67
  - Executive Positions 68
    - The Captain 68
    - The Co-Pilot 69
  - Assigning Executive Positions 69
  - Crew Flight Positions 70
- Awareness of Abilities 71
- Monitoring and Appraisal 72
  - Personal Performance 72
  - Professional Monitoring 72
  - Active monitoring 73
  - Monitoring Styles 73
  - Monitoring and the Cockpit Gradient 74
  - Positive Communication 75
  - Asserting Yourself 75
- Intercom Protocols 75
- Managing Workloads 76
- Effective Leadership and Authority 78
- Effectively Applying Standards 80
- Monitoring and Maintaining Performance 82
  - Maintaining Situational Awareness 85
  - Make Effective Decisions 86
  - Resource Allocation 87
- Preparation for Practical Lessons 88
- Standard Operating Procedures (SOPs) 90
  - What to Standardise 90
  - MCC Roles and Responsibilities 91
  - FP / PM Roles 92
  - PF / PM Responsibilities 93
  - MCC Checklists 93
  - Using the Checklist 94
  - Checklist Conventions 96
  - Checklist Response 97
  - Completing a Checklist 97
  - Checklist Verbal Procedures 99
  - MCC Standard Words and Phrases 101
  - Using the Radio in an MCC Environment 104

MCC Standard Procedures 106
Handover Takeover Procedure 106
The Lookout Procedure.. 108
The Hot Swap Procedure 109
Altimeter QNH Setting Procedure 109
Altitude Alert Setting Procedure 110
Radio Altimeter Setting Procedure 111
Flight Guidance and Navigation System Setting Procedure 112

Appendices 114
Appendix 1: Example STAR Checklist 114
Appendix 2: Improved Aeronautical Decision Making Can Reduce Accidents 118
Appendix 3: Air Ambulance Strikes Terrain After Takeoff in Fog 124

Terms and Abbreviations 128
Bibliography 129

About this Book

While common in the airline industry, Multi-Crew Cooperation is only now becoming better understood in the helicopter industry as larger and more sophisticated helicopters become available and high-intensity operations, including NVG and IFR, become increasingly common in the helicopter working environment. This book explains Crew Resource Management, Threat and Error Management and Multi-Crew Cooperation specific to the helicopter operating environment.

"Multi-Crew Cooperation for Helicopter Pilots" is written by Captain Mike Becker, one of Australia's most experienced helicopter instructors. Mike Becker started flying in 1984. His career has been as diverse as the number of helicopter types he has flown – the smaller R22 to the larger B212 and Sikorski S62, and most types in between. He is experienced in a vast range of helicopter operations, including high altitude, remote area operations, mustering, firefighting, tourism, sling load operations, specialised long line operations, search and rescue, and Night Vision Goggles operations.

He has been operating a helicopter flight school since 1995. As Chief Pilot and Chief Flight Instructor, Mike operated a fleet of over 20 helicopters and employed more than 30 instructors delivering over 10,000 training hours per year.

With over 16,000 flight hours and the recipient of the "Captain John Ashton Award for Flight Standards and Aviation Safety" by the Guild of Air Pilots and Air Navigators of London, Mike's experience provides invaluable insights and real hands-on knowledge.

This theory book converts all this experience and those of his instructional staff into a practical, hands-on guide.

"Multi-Crew Cooperation" teaches practical techniques to maximise safety margins, promote team coordination in the constantly changing environment of helicopter flight operations.

About the Author

Mike Becker is one of Australia's most experienced helicopter instructors, with over 16,000 hours of rotary-wing flight experience. His career has taken him from the mountains in New Zealand to the outback of Australia and the jungles of Papua New Guinea. He has also worked in the United States, Italy and Borneo.

He has flown a range of helicopter types – the Robinson R22, Robinson R44, Bell 47, Hughes 269, Hughes 500, Bell 206, Bell 427, Bell 212, EC120, Dragon Fly, Brantley B2B, Enstrom EF28, Sikorsky S62A, Hiller H12ET, Aerospatial AS350, Agusta 109E Power, Agusta 109S Grand, and the Agusta 119 Koala.

He is experienced in a comprehensive range of helicopter operations, including high altitude, remote area operations, mustering, firefighting, tourism, sling load operations, specialised long-line operations, search and rescue, and Night Vision Goggles operations.

Mike is a Grade One Flight Instructor and Flight Examiner who holds an Australian Air Transport Pilots Licence (Helicopter) and an Australian Commercial Pilots Licence (Fixed Wing).

Mike is the Chief Pilot and Head of Training for his own business Becker Helicopters, in Australia. He, and his wife Jan, established Becker Helicopters in 1997 with one Bell 47 and have grown the company through a love of helicopters, hard work, and determination.

Mike is the recipient of many awards, including the "Captain John Ashton Award for Flight Standards and Aviation Safety" by the Guild of Air Pilots and Air Navigators of London, which was awarded in recognition of over 18,000 accident-free flight training hours at Becker Helicopters. Mike has also authored "Mike Becker's Helicopter Handbook", first published in 1986, and a range of theory books and instructional videos.

Multi-Crew Cooperation *for Helicopter Pilots*

Introduction

Multi-Crew Cooperation (MCC) training is a relatively new term for helicopter operators. Much of the MCC training has been conducted for some time under the guise of Crew Resource Management (CRM). However, typically CRM did not specifically focus on the coordination and procedures used by two (2) pilots actually flying the helicopter. Instead, it looked at a holistic approach to the Pilot In Command managing any internal and external cockpit resources that were available to assist and manage the flight. MCC training addresses this shortfall and focuses on the two flying pilots.

MCC training is only widespread in the airline industry, where multi-crew is the normal way to operate a large airliner. Still, it is only now becoming more understood in the helicopter industry as bigger and more sophisticated helicopters are becoming available and high-intensity operations, including NVG and IFR, become more common in the helicopter working environment.

Pyramid of Training

MCC training represents the pinnacle in a pyramid of training for two (2) pilot operations.

The entire MCC training package is usually delivered over a period of time as each pilot will focus on the various layers in the pyramid while gaining and building knowledge and experience as they advance into more complex aircraft types and operations.

Each layer of the pyramid represents a competency, and specific skill sets that are acquired until the pilot is finally eligible to receive the MCC portion.

Who it applies to

This applies to any pilot who is required to operate in a multi-crew environment regardless of whether the aircraft is certified for multi-crew operations or not.

Building blocks

Each layer in the pyramid of training represents a building block of knowledge, skill and behaviour that the pilot will develop over time by completing courses and attaining licences.

Foundation Aviation Knowledge and Airmanship

The Foundation Aviation Knowledge and Airmanship forms the base of the pyramid and represents the previous core Knowledge, Skills and Behaviours learnt during the training for a PPL, CPL, ATPL or equivalent (military) course.

Of particular importance is the knowledge relating to:

- Airmanship (built on during a pilot's entire career)
- Aeromedical factors
- Human Factors

Risk Management

Understanding the principles of Risk Management allows risk management strategies to be applied to aviation.

This includes:

- Identifying risks
- Assessing Risks
- Managing risks
- Applying risk management to aviation

Threat Error Management (TEM)

Threat and Error Management is the process of applying Risk Management strategies to the flying environment.

This includes:

- Threat identification and management
- Error identification and management
- Undesired aircraft state identification and management
- Mitigating strategies or countermeasures which link back to Risk Management and forward to Crew Resource Management

Crew Resource Management (CRM)

CRM applies systems and strategies to allow teams to work together as a whole.

This includes:

- Situational awareness
- Communication
- Leadership/Followership and working as a team
- Problem-solving, decision making and judgment
- Task / Workload management
- Briefings

Multi-crew Operations

MCC Operations is the culmination of the above four pieces of the pyramid where the two pilots in the cockpit now operate within set Standard Operating Procedures for a particular aircraft type in order to safely operate the aircraft. Therefore, MCC is seen as the pinnacle of training and sits at the top of the pyramid of knowledge for a pilot.

MCC includes:

- Use of a standard phraseology
- Use of Standard Operating Procedures (SOPs) for a specific aircraft type
- Use of aircraft type-specific checklists
- The ability to assess cockpit workloads and priorities to optimise the available capacity
- The delegation of tasks and workload management in accordance with the SOPs for a specific aircraft type

Multi-Crew Cooperation *for Helicopter Pilots*

Introduction to This Book

This book builds on the foundation aviation knowledge and airmanship and discusses the requirements in the upper layers of the pyramid, including risk management, threat error management, crew resource management and finally, multi-crew cooperation.

It is important to note that this book assumes that each pilot in the cockpit is a fully licenced pilot with a Private Pilots licence or higher. It is not designed for aircrew completing some pilot duties and tasks that may be approved for some Helicopter Emergency Medical (HEM) operators in Australia.

In saying that, this book will also be useful and applicable to aircrew completing limited pilot duties in an MCC operation, but the book would have to be modified not to include any actual flying duties by the aircrew member.

Risk Management

Risk management has long been the backbone of aviation operations and, particularly, Safety Management Systems to identify hazards and mitigate (reduce or eliminate) the risk of that hazard occurring. It is one of the first steps by an operator to identify and develop strategies to manage the aviation hazards associated with its operation.

What is Risk?

Risk is defined as *"the chance or possibility of something happening that could have an impact on the desired outcome."*

Risk Management

Risk Management is the sum of the coordinated activities an organisation does to direct and control risk (AS/NZS ISO 31000:2009). Risk management aims to make sure risks are identified and managed to an acceptable level.

Why pilots?

As a pilot, it is essential to have an understanding of the principles of risk management, both in terms of understanding an operator's risk management systems and risk mitigators (this includes the policies, processes and actions put into place to minimise a particular risk) as well as to be able to apply the principles of risk management to flight operations.

An understanding of the principles of risk management leads to effective:

- Threat Error Management
- Crew Resource Management, and
- Multi-Crew Co-operation practices.

Key Components

A Risk Management System involves two (2) fundamental activities:

1. Identifying hazards:
   Situations or conditions that may lead to incidents and accidents.
2. Assessing (analysing) and mitigating the risks:
   Methods or practices to reduce or eliminate the hazard to prevent incidents and accidents.

The Process

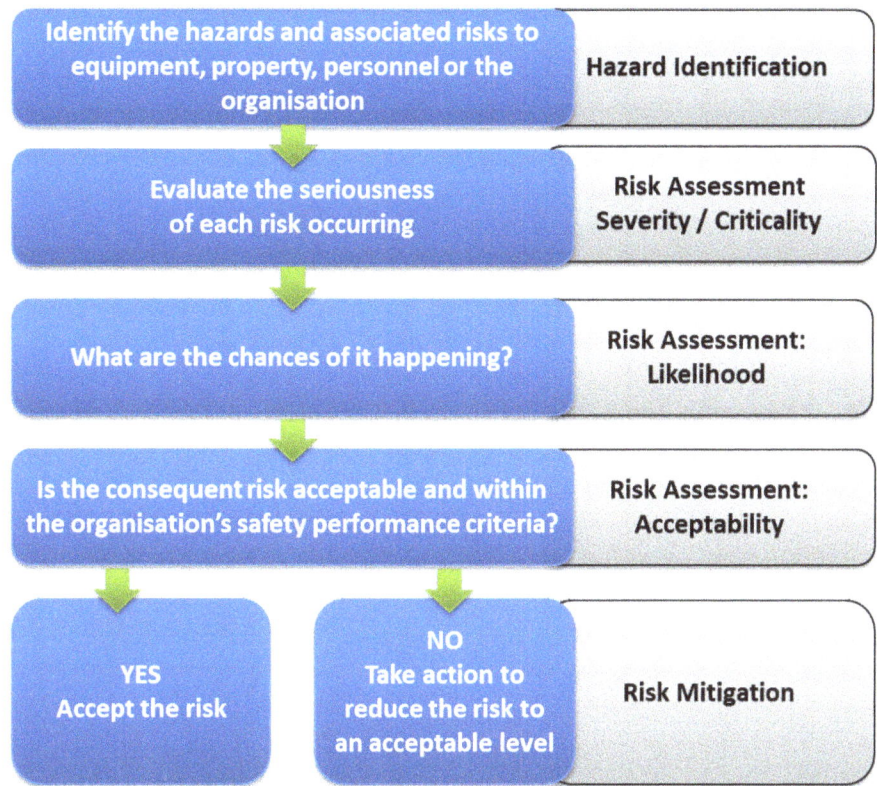

Key Definitions

To understand risk management, we need to understand what a *hazard* is and then relate this to the *risk* and then to the *management* of the risk.

Hazard

A **hazard** is an event or a situation that could result in damage, injury or a dangerous outcome.

Risk

A **risk** is the chance of something happening that could impact a desired outcome. It could be either a positive or negative risk.

Risk is measured in terms of the consequence versus the likelihood of the event.

Risk = Likelihood x Consequence

In aviation, we tend only to consider the negative aspects of risk related to the safety of the flight.

Mitigation

Mitigation is the measures taken to eliminate a hazard or reduce the likelihood or severity of a risk.

Management

Management is the act of collating all the relevant information and resources (including people) and then putting this together to accomplish a desired goal or objective.

Management encompasses planning, organising, resourcing, staffing, leading, directing and controlling an organisation or group or effort to accomplish a goal.

> **Example**

Consider the image below. What are the hazard and the risk, and how could this be managed?

The *hazard* is getting bitten by the snake.

The *risk* is getting bitten by the snake is highly likely if there is no barrier between the snake and visitors.

The *mitigation* is putting the snake behind a glass barrier.

The *management* process is identifying the hazard, assessing the likelihood and consequences of the hazard and determining effective methods to mitigate the risk. In this case, putting the snake into a sealed cage significantly reduces the likelihood of visitors being bitten by the snake.

Identifying Hazards

The first part of any risk management process is to identify the hazards. Only when a hazard has been identified can you determine the best way to eliminate or reduce the risk. Different types of hazards need to be considered.

Visible hazards

Visible hazards are usually obvious; they can be easily seen, smelt, heard, tasted, or felt. Examples in aviation may include a faulty light or a rough-running engine.

Hidden hazards

Hidden hazards can include physical hazards such as electricity and radiation and hazards such as inadequate training, stress, system failure, and the effects of altitude.

Emerging hazards

Emerging hazards are hazards that initially seem minor and do not receive attention but soon become worse and could cause significant damage, such as a tiny oil leak or an issue with teamwork amongst crew members.

Methods to identify

There are many ways to identify hazards; some include:

- Task Analysis
- Brainstorming
- SWOT analysis
- Risk Dimension Analysis
- Workplace inspections
- Interviews with staff
- Surveys
- Safety meetings
- Checklists
- Audits
- Safety investigations
- Hazard reports
- Audit reports
- Review and analysis of incident and other safety reports
- Injury and illness history
- Industry data and experience
- Information from similar organisations.

Structured approach

It is important to take a structured approach to identify hazards to reduce the chance of missing something. More than one method of identifying hazards may be used. Past hazard and incident reports is one of the most important sources of hazard information. Brainstorming may also highlight new emerging hazards.

What to consider

When identifying hazards, you would consider:

- Who (stakeholders) needs to be involved.
  For example, include ground staff, senior staff and less experienced staff to give a broader perspective.
- Consider all aspects.
  For example, aircraft, equipment, human factors, environmental factors, organisational, how busy we are, and even what changes are taking place.

Key questions

When identifying hazards, keep asking yourself:

- What can happen?
- How can it happen?
- Why could it happen?
- When could it happen?
- Where could it happen?

Document the hazards

Record each of the hazards identified into a register, and identify:

- the hazard
- what current controls there are to reduce the risk of this hazard occurring.

Risk Assessment (Analysis)

What next

Once hazards are identified, they need to be assessed. To analyse the risk, determine:

- What is the consequence of this risk?
- What is the likelihood of this risk occurring?

Consequence

Each organisation may define its own way of determining the consequence level.

The consequence level may consider:

- Injury to staff or the public
- Loss of aircraft/equipment
- Publicity and the impact on reputation and client confidence
- Financial risk, etc.

Each hazard is then rated based on its level of consequence as follows:

Catastrophic	One or more fatalities. Loss of aircraft or major equipment. Resulting in negative publicity involving video coverage (TV or internet).
Critical	Serious injury to one or more people, resulting in permanent disability. Sustained or extensive damage to aircraft or equipment. Resulting in negative publicity involving print only (no video coverage).
Major	Injury that requires hospitalisation (with no permanent disability) Damage to aircraft/ equipment resulting in temporary inability to use it.
Moderate	Injury requiring only First Aid (no permanent disability). Isolated and quickly-repaired damage to aircraft.
Minor	No injury or very minor injury that does not require First Aid. Minor or no damage to aircraft or equipment.

Likelihood

Each hazard is then rated on the likelihood of it occurring as follows:

Likely	Expected to occur at least once during the task or activity.
Probable	Could occur during the task or activity.
Possible	It's conceivable it could occur, but only expected infrequently.
Unlikely	It's conceivable that this could happen, although only in unusual circumstances.
Rare	It's not conceivable that this could occur.

Risk matrix

By combining the Consequence with the Likelihood, a **Risk Matrix** can be created.

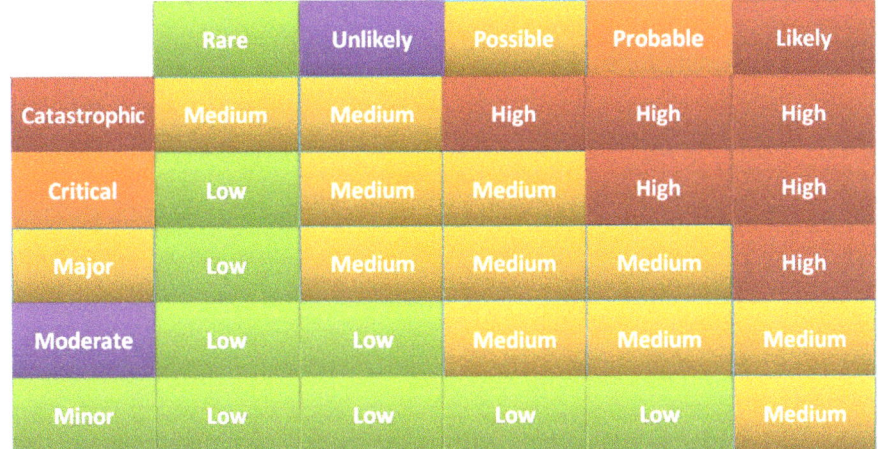

Risk level

For each hazard, based on the consequence and likelihood rating, you can determine the risk level for each hazard as follows:

HIGH

Considerable potential for fatalities or serious injuries or the loss of an aircraft or equipment.

MEDIUM

Moderate potential for injuries requiring hospitalisation or the damage of an aircraft or equipment.

LOW

Minimal potential for injuries (above those requiring First Aid) or for any consequential damage to aircraft or equipment.

What next

Once assessing each hazard, prioritise the risks from highest to lowest, and then consider how to treat each risk.

Controlling the Risk: Risk Mitigation

Once you have identified the hazards and assessed the risk in terms of consequence and likelihood, it is time to consider ways to mitigate (reduce or eliminate) the risk.

Risk treatment

You can consider different actions or design resources that will reduce the consequence of a risk, the likelihood of a risk, or both.

Strategy

When considering methods to control the risk, you may consider methods to:

- Avoid the risk by adopting a different way of doing something or choosing to no longer conduct an activity because it is deemed too high a risk.
- Reduce the risk – identify ways to reduce the risk through controls, etc.
- Share the risk – get someone to share the responsibility for the risk.
- Refer the risk – get someone else to treat the risk, for example, asking a supplier to reduce the risk of a hazard associated with a piece of equipment, or
- Retain the risk – decide to carry the risk that remains.

What to consider

When considering ways to mitigate the risk, consider:

- Human Factors: health, stress management, fatigue, experience levels, workload.
- Aircraft and equipment: lighting, labels, instrumentation, automation, etc.
- Environment: weather, terrain, airport, airspace, night-time, visual illusions.
- External pressures.

Methods to mitigate

When considering methods to mitigate the risk, you may consider:

- Limitations or restrictions: Limiting a task to only multi-crew operations
- Procedures: Use of checklists (create or modify checklists)
- Equipment: Modify equipment/aircraft to reduce the risk; for example, put a protective shield over a dangerous item, colour code items, add new lighting or change labels to give clearer meaning.
- Training: Modify or add training to provide greater awareness and training in a procedure.

One or more methods may be combined to reduce the risk.

Be aware

Beware that mitigation may introduce new hazards or risks to the operation. For example, new lighting may prove distracting or confusing and not achieve the original aim.

Be realistic

Not all mitigation is appropriate. For instance, it is not wise to expect consistent, error-free human performance as the only way to prevent an accident.

Challenge the team to determine whether the mitigation they propose is realistic given what they know about people, equipment and operations. If there is doubt, have them consider what else can be done.

Consistent results

A mitigation method may not be effective all the time and, therefore, may require more than one mitigation treatment.

Challenge and test

The team should challenge and test whether the mitigation proposed will be effective. This may involve brainstorming scenarios in which these mitigation approaches are implemented.

Be practical

It may not be practical to expect that a high amount of resources (in terms of people or expenditure) be applied to mitigate a risk. Sometimes a simple checklist can be as effective as sophisticated automation at a fraction of the cost.

Case Study: Risk Assessment Checklist

Becker Helicopters uses a *S.T.A.R.* checklist to assess the risks for a particular task. **STAR** stands for:

S_{TOP}, T_{HINK}, A_{SSESS and} R_{ATE}.

An example of a STAR checklist is provided in Appendix 1: Example STAR Checklist.

Threat Error Management

Threat Error Management (TEM) is a relatively new title for something aviators have been doing for a long time but have not formally articulated or discussed as a crew. TEM involves:

- identifying any threats both external to the aircraft and internal to the aircraft
- identifying any possible areas for the crew and others to make errors
- putting a strategy in place to manage these threats and errors.

Preparation and mentoring

Having the crew identify and verbalise threats and errors allows the instructor to mentor and the trainee to learn what to look for regarding threats and errors.

Before take-off, it brings to the front of the crew's mind those areas that could pose a problem and allows solutions to be thought of before the event.

TEM Principles and Model

CASA definition

Threat and Error Management (TEM): The process of detecting and responding to threats and errors to ensure that the ensuing outcome is inconsequential.

That is, the outcome is not an error, further error or undesired state.

ICAO definition

The Threat and Error Management (TEM) framework is a conceptual model that assists in understanding, from an operational perspective, the inter-relationship between safety and human performance in dynamic and challenging operational contexts.

Basis of TEM

The fundamental premise of Threat and Error Management is that threats and errors are unavoidable components of complex operational environments. Therefore, the basis of TEM is managing threats and errors rather than avoiding or eliminating them.

Errors are common

One common yet false assumption is that errors and violations are limited to incidents and accidents. Recent data from Flight Operations Monitoring (e.g., LOSA) indicate that errors and violations are quite common during flight operations.

According to the University of Texas LOSA database:

- In around 60% of the flights, at least one error or violation was observed, the average per flight being 1.5 errors.
- A quarter of the errors and violations were mismanaged or had consequences (an undesired aircraft state or another error).
- A third of the errors were detected and corrected by the flight crew, 4% were detected but made worse, and over 60% of errors remained undetected.
- This data should underline the fact that errors are normal during flight operations and that, as such, they are usually not immediately dangerous.

TEM Model

Since we are only human, threats and errors will always be a part of every flight, so effectively managing them is critical to ensuring they don't escalate into an undesired aircraft state or, worse, a fatal accident.

The TEM model is a framework that helps to manage this by understanding, from an operational perspective, the relationship between safety and human performance in an aviation environment. It categorises the major factors in the accident chain of events and takes into consideration external factors, human errors, crew responses, undesired aircraft states and likely outcomes and identifies opportunities for countermeasures.

There are three basic categories in the TEM model, they are:

- Threats
- Errors
- Undesired aircraft state

The following model from the 2005 Qantas Airways Command course illustrates these categories within a TEM framework.

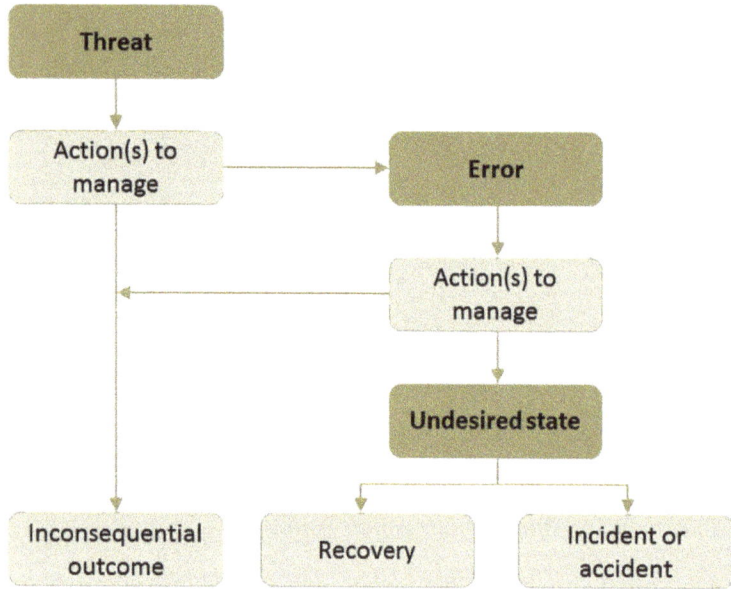

On any given flight, the flight crew will encounter a number of **threats** that may or may not require a response to maintain safety. For example, bad weather, maintenance unserviceability, non-standard phraseology, fatigue and hazardous attitudes.

The flight crew will have strategies to manage these threats, for example, well-practised standard operating procedures (SOPs). However, some will require the crew to use decision-making skills and troubleshoot solutions. The model implies, however, that if the strategies used to deal with the threat are inadequate, then **errors** may occur. For example, not confirming ATC clearance or setting incorrect altitude.

It should be noted that while threats can lead to errors, errors can happen regardless.

If the error management is adequate and resolved, either by aircraft equipment (e.g., ground proximity warning systems, checklists, SOPs, etc.) or human responses (e.g., decision making, leadership, situational awareness, vigilance, monitoring and cross-checking), then the error will lead to an inconsequential outcome.

However, if the error management is inadequate, it can lead to an **undesired aircraft state,** such as an unstabilised approach resulting in either recovery or accident.

TEM philosophy

Flight crew should manage threats pro-actively, so they have time to think through alternative strategies and 'capture' errors before they have adverse consequences.

The TEM philosophy stresses three basic concepts:

- *anticipation*
- recognition
- recovery.

The key to anticipation is accepting that while something is likely to go wrong, you can't know what it will be or when it will happen.

Hence, a chronic unease reinforces the vigilance necessary in all safety-critical professions. Anticipation builds vigilance, and vigilance is the key to recognizing adverse events and errors.

Logically, recognition leads to recovery. In some cases, particularly when an error escalates to an undesired aircraft state, recovering adequate safety margins is the first line of action: **Recover first, analyse the causes later**.

Summary

If you consider a normal flight, to manage operational goals while maintaining flight safety, the crew must:

- Manage everyday operational problems – referred to as Threat Management
- Manage their own errors – referred to as Error Management
- Manage unsafe situations – referred to as Undesired Aircraft States

The key to threat error management is teaching pilots practical techniques to maximise safety margins and promote anticipation or 'thinking ahead' in the constantly changing environment of flight operations.

Threats and Threat Management

Definition

Threats are everywhere during flight operations, from adverse weather and airport conditions to ATC and aircraft malfunctions. Flight crews must divert their attention from normal flight duties to manage them and the more complex or challenging the operating environment becomes, the greater the flight crew's workload.

A threat can be defined as:

- A situation or event that has the potential to impact negatively on the safety of a flight, or
- Any influence that promotes opportunity for pilot error(s).

Categories

Threats can be divided into the following categories:

1. External Threats
2. Internal Threats

External Threats

External threats include anything **"external"** to the aircraft but that the flight crew will interact with during the flight.

You are, in effect, looking at any threats that are external to you but that can affect you. This includes both environmental threats and organisational threats, for example:

Examples of Environmental Threats

Environmental Threats	Examples
Adverse weather	Thunderstorms, turbulence, poor visibility, wind shear, icing conditions, IMC
Airport	Congested parking bays, taxiways and helipads, proximity to open hangars and parked aircraft. Conflict with fixed-wing, lack of, confusing, or faded signage and markings, moving security, refuelling and other ground vehicles. Birds, unserviceable navigation aids, complex surface-navigation procedures, airport constructions, fly neighbourly policies, FOD, designated local training areas, lighting, etc.
ATC	Other traffic, ATC error, ATC language accent, ATC speaking too fast or too quiet, ATS using non-standard phraseology, ATC not confirming or correcting readbacks, ATC runway changes, ATIS/AWIS changes and differences, confusion in units of measurement (feet vs meters, QNH vs QFE), transponder codes and the use of the transponder, etc.
Environmental operational pressure	Terrain, traffic, radio congestion

Examples of Operational Threats

Operational Threats	Examples
Aircraft	Aircraft not available, aircraft not prepared or ready, aircraft malfunctions and snags, starting issues, MEL and Maintenance Release issues, aircraft not configured correctly (no dual controls), etc.
Operational pressure	Delays, late arrivals, aircraft and equipment changes, refuelling issues, etc.
Cabin	Lack of cabin and baggage security, flight crew error, cabin event distraction, interruption, cabin door security.
Maintenance	Maintenance not completed, acceptance after maintenance not completed, helicopter still in maintenance, paperwork after maintenance not completed, maintenance error etc.
Ground	Ground handling event, dirty windows and fuselage, aircraft not left secured, ground crew error, FOD left in the vicinity of the aircraft, etc.
Dispatch	Dispatch paperwork event or error, aircraft allocation, etc.
Documentation	Chart error, flight plan error, incorrect aircraft documentation received.
Other	Crew scheduling event where flight and duty times are extended or exceeded, trainees not being prepared or ready for the flight, crew influenced by drugs or alcohol, etc.

Types

There are generally three types of external threats:

- Expected
- Unexpected
- Latent

Expected external threats

Some threats can be anticipated since they are expected or known to the flight crew. For example, flight crews can anticipate the consequences of a thunderstorm by briefing their response in advance or prepare for a congested airport by making sure they keep a watchful eye for other aircraft as they execute the approach.

Unexpected external threats

Some threats can occur unexpectedly, such as an in-flight aircraft malfunction that happens suddenly and without warning. In this case, flight crews must apply skills and knowledge acquired through training and operational experience to manage the threat.

Latent external threats

Some threats may not be directly obvious to or observable by flight crews immersed in the operational context and may need to be uncovered by safety analyses. These are considered latent threats.

Examples of latent threats include:

- equipment design issues
- optical illusions
- shortened turn-around schedules.

Internal Threats

Internal threats are those arising from the *flight crew* themselves and may include:

Internal Threats	Examples
Fatigue	Flight duty times at night or other times of the day when you would normally be sleeping.
Team familiarity	How well you know your flight crew colleagues, whether you have flown together before. Too much familiarity can produce problems, just as too little can.
Language and culture issues	Organisational, professional, national and cultural differences.
Health and Fitness	Whether you report for duty feeling capable of doing the job. This can be affected by illness, lack of sleep, substance abuse, hangovers etc.
Experience	Lack of experience in a role can impose a threat just as too much experience can be a threat due to complacency.
Operational recency and proficiency	This means being 'current' or up-to-date and 'practised' at performing specific procedures of flying certain routes. Absence from flying for an extended period of time can cause your familiarity with, and competence in that role, to be reduced.

Knowledge and Familiarity

When flight crews lack both knowledge and familiarity/experience with the operation, they tend to make more errors and mismanage those errors at a greater rate. However, a sound knowledge of the operation still does not guarantee that a flight crew won't make mistakes. But good operational knowledge and familiarity will result in fewer mistakes, fewer serious mistakes, and more quickly discovered and corrected ones than those made by pilots without sufficient knowledge.

Threat Management

Threat management

Threat management can be broadly defined as how crews anticipate and/or respond to threats.

A mismanaged threat is defined as a threat that is linked to or induces flight crew errors.

Tools and techniques

Some of the common tools and techniques used in commercial aviation to manage threats and prevent crew errors include:

- The use of **S**tandard **O**perating **P**rocedures (**SOP**s)
- Pre-flight crew briefings
- Reading weather and NOTAM information
- Use of **S**afety **M**anagement **S**ystems (**SMS**) so that information is shared within organisations
- Thorough pre-flight inspections and a pre-departure walk around
- Correct use of Checklists and procedures to diagnose unexpected aircraft malfunctions and emergencies.

Errors and Error Management

Put simply, threats come **"at"** the crew, while errors come **"from"** the crew.

Errors are defined as flight crew actions or inactions that:

- lead to a deviation from crew or organisational intentions or expectations
- reduce safety margins
- increase the probability of adverse operational events on the ground or during flight.

Errors can be:

- spontaneous and independent of a threat (e.g., incorrectly setting an altitude)
- induced by a threat that was not countered (e.g., missing a checklist item due to a radio call interruption)
- a link in a chain of errors – with each compounding the problem (e.g., iced pitot head, leading to airspeed error, leading to incorrect pilot actions, leading to an extreme attitude and airspeed).

Categories of errors

Flight crew errors can be divided into three categories:

1. Aircraft Handling Errors
2. Procedural Errors
3. Communication Errors

Errors	Examples
Aircraft Handling Errors	- Manual handling/flight controls: vertical/lateral and/or speed deviations. - Automation: incorrect altitude, speed, heading, autothrottle settings, incorrect mode executed, or incorrect entries. - Systems/radio/instruments: incorrect packs, incorrect anti-icing, incorrect altimeter, incorrect fuel switches settings, incorrect speed bug, incorrect radio frequency dialled. - Ground navigation: attempting to turn down the wrong taxiway/runway, taxi too fast, failure to hold short, missed taxiway/runway.
Procedural Errors	- SOPs: failure to cross-check settings. - Checklists: wrong challenge and response; items missed, checklist performed late or at the wrong time. - Callouts: omitted/incorrect callouts - Briefings: items missed in the brief, omitted departure, takeoff, approach or handover briefing. - Documentation: wrong weight and balance, fuel infomation, ATIS, or clearance information recorded, misinterpreted items on paperwork, incorrect logbook entries, incorrect application of MEL procedures.
Communication Errors	- Crew to external: missed calls, misinterpretations of instructions, incorrect read-back, wrong clearance, taxiway, gate or runway communicated. - Pilot to pilot: within crew miscommunication or misinterpretation

Human Error

Human error is cited as a causal or contributing factor in the majority of aviation occurrences. Errors are not some type of aberrant behaviour; they are a natural by-product of virtually all human endeavours. Therefore, error must be accepted as a normal component of any system where humans and technology interact.

"To err is human."

To deal with human error is "management" – safety management!

Slips, Lapses and Intentional

Flight crew errors can be the result of the momentary diversion of attention (slip) or memory failure (lapse) induced by an expected or unexpected threat. Other errors are more deliberate and are known as intentional non-compliance errors. These are often shortcuts used by flight crews to increase operational efficiency, though they are in violation of standard operating procedures.

Errors versus Violations

Errors, which are normal human activity, are quite distinct from violations. However, both can lead to a failure of the system, and both can result in a hazardous situation. The difference between errors and violations lies in the intent. A violation in this context is a deliberate act, while an error is unintentional.

Some violations are the result of poor or unrealistic procedures where people have developed "workarounds" to accomplish the task. In such cases, they must be reported as soon as they are encountered so the procedures can be corrected. In any event, violations should not be tolerated.

There have been accidents where a corporate culture that tolerated or, in some cases, encouraged the taking of short-cuts rather than the following of published procedures, was identified as a contributory cause.

Violation - Deliberate act contrary to a procedure or a "workaround"

Error Management

How was the error managed?

Understanding how the error was managed is as important, if not more important, than understanding the prevalence of different types of errors. It is of interest to know if and when the error was detected and by whom, as well as the response(s) upon detecting the error and the outcome or consequence of the error.

As with threats, some errors are quickly detected and resolved leading to inconsequential outcomes, while others go undetected or are mismanaged.

Regardless of the cause or severity, the outcome of an error depends on whether the flight crew detects and manages the error before it leads to an undesired aircraft state and a potentially unsafe outcome. This is why the foundation of TEM lies in understanding error management rather than solely focusing on the error occurrence (Maurino, 2006)[1]. Fortunately, few errors lead to adverse consequences, let alone accidents. Typically, errors are identified and corrected with no undesirable outcomes.

On the understanding that errors are normal in human behaviours, however, the total elimination of human error would be an unrealistic goal. The challenge then is not merely to prevent errors but to learn to safely manage the inevitable errors.

Error management is an important part of safety management.

Undetected errors

Approximately 45% of the observed errors are errors that go undetected or that are not responded to by the flight crew.

An important point for effective error management: An error that is not detected cannot be managed.

Error Management Strategies

Strategies for error management include:

- error reduction
- error capturing
- error tolerance.

---

[1] Maurino, D. (2005). Threat and Error Management (TEM). Canadian Aviation Safety Seminar (CASS). Vancouver, Canada, 18-20 April 2005. See: https://www.skybrary.aero/bookshelf/books/515.pdf

Error reduction - reduce or eliminate the contributing factors

Error reduction strategies intervene directly at the source of the error by reducing or eliminating the contributing factors that trigger the error.

Error capturing – "capture" the error before any adverse consequences of the error are felt

Error capturing assumes the error has already been made. The intent is to "capture" the error before any adverse consequences of the error are felt. Error capturing is dfferent from error reduction in that it does not directly serve to reduce or eliminate the error, just to manage its consequence.

Error tolerance – system ability to accept error

Error tolerance refers to the ability of a system to accept an error without serious consequence.

Error outcomes

Depending on the response to the error, there are three possible error outcomes:

- **Inconsequential**: the error does not affect the safe completion of the flight or was made irrelevant by successful cockpit crew error management. This is the most common outcome.
- **Undesired aircraft state**: is defined as a position, condition or attitude of an aircraft that clearly reduces safety margins and is a result of actions by the flight crew. The error results in the aircraft being unnecessarily placed in a condition that increases risk. This includes incorrect vertical or lateral navigation, unstable approaches, low fuel state, lining up for the wrong runway and reduced separation.
- **Additional Error**: An error by the flight crew that now needs to be managed

Mis-managed error

An error that is detected and effectively managed has no adverse impact on the flight. On the other hand, a mismanaged error reduces safety margins by linking to or inducing additional error or an undesired aircraft state.

Undesired Aircraft State

Definition

Unfortunately, not all errors are well managed. Sometimes they lead to another error, or a safety-compromising event called an **U**ndesired **A**ircraft **S**tate (**UAS**). An undesired aircraft state (UAS) is defined as a position, condition or attitude of an aircraft that clearly reduces safety margins and is a result of actions by the flight crew (Merritt & Klinect, 2006)[2]. It is a safety compromising state that results from ineffective error management.

UAS	Examples
Aircraft handling	<ul><li>Aircraft control (excessive pitch or roll attitude).</li><li>Vertical, lateral or speed deviations. (excessive IAS, VSI)</li><li>Unnecessary weather penetration (turbulence).</li><li>Unauthorized airspace penetration.</li><li>Operation outside aircraft limitations (exceeding power limits, RPM limits, weight limits)</li><li>Unstable approach (VRS, overpitching, operating in the Deadman's curve)</li><li>Continued landing after an unstable approach (overshooting or undershooting)</li><li>Hard landing</li></ul>
Ground navigation	<ul><li>Proceeding towards the wrong taxiway, runway or HLS</li></ul>

---

[2] Merritt, A. and Klinect, J. (2006). Defensive Flying for Pilots: An Introduction to Threat and Error Management. The University of Texas Human Factors Research Project, The LOSA Collaborative. See: https://www.skybrary.aero/bookshelf/ books/1982.pdf

UAS	Examples
Incorrect aircraft configurations	- Incorrect systems configuration - Incorrect flight controls configuration - Incorrect automation configuration - Incorrect engine configuration - Incorrect weight and balance configuration

UAS management

As with errors, UAS can be managed effectively, returning the aircraft to safe flight; or flight crew action or inaction can induce an additional error or result in an incident or accident. A UAS is often considered at the cusp of becoming an incident or accident and, therefore, must be managed by flight crews.

Primacy of UAS management

It is important to understand that UAS management has primacy over 'error' or 'threat' management.

That is, the Undesired Aircraft State should be managed before managing an error or threat.

The crew should avoid getting locked into the error management phase.

Example

A flight crew selects the wrong approach in the Flight Management Computer (FMC).

The flight crew subsequently identifies the error during a crosscheck before the Final Approach Fix (FAF). However, instead of using a basic mode (e.g., heading) or manually flying the desired track, both flight crew become involved in attempting to reprogram the correct approach before reaching the FAF.

As a result, the aircraft "stitches" through the localiser, descends late and goes into an unstable approach.

This would be an example of the flight crew getting "locked in" to error management rather than switching to undesired aircraft state management.

Outcomes and UAS

It is also important to establish a clear differentiation between undesired aircraft states and outcomes.

Undesired aircraft states are transitional states between a normal operational state (i.e., a stabilised approach) and an outcome. While at the undesired aircraft state stage, the flight crew has the possibility, through appropriate TEM, of recovering the situation and returning to a normal operational state, thus restoring margins of safety.

Outcomes, on the other hand, are end states, most notably, reportable occurrences (i.e., incidents and accidents). Once the undesired aircraft state becomes an outcome, recovery of the situation, return to a normal operational state, and restoration of margins of safety is not possible.

For example, a stabilised approach (normal operational state) turns into an unstabilised approach (undesired aircraft state) that results in a runway excursion (outcome).

Application of TEM

The TEM model can be a useful tool not just for flight crew but the organisation as a whole. Some practical applications include using it as a:

- training tool
- reporting tool for incidents
- systematic observation tool
- proactive analysis tool.

Training Tool

As a training tool, TEM can help individuals clarify their performance needs and vulnerabilities from a different perspective. This is particularly relevant in Human Factors training programs; indeed, ICAO has adopted the TEM model in its Human Factors Training Manual (ICAO Document 9683)[3].

Reporting Tool

When reporting on an incident, the TEM format prompts pilots to report information about the threats that were present, the errors they may have made, how well the event was managed and how the event may have been avoided or handled better.

Systematic Observation

The TEM model was first conceived in conjunction with the development of the LOSA program, a behavioural audit methodology that studies flight crew threat and error management capabilities during normal flight operations. Therefore, its original application was as an observation tool. Feasibility studies are currently underway to explore the transfer of the methodology to other operational areas within aviation such as airline flight dispatch, air traffic control and cabin crew.

Proactive Analysis

When TEM is used as the framework for safety data collection, a wealth of information can be extracted. An organisation can use the data to understand patterns at the organisational level. The data can also be collected across the industry and analysed for systemic trends.

Countermeasures

Countermeasures

Countermeasures are tools and techniques to help anticipate, recognise and recover from threats, errors and undesired aircraft states. They may also be called safeguards. Examples of countermeasures include checklists, briefings, call-outs and SOPs as well as personal strategies and tactics.

According to Merritt and Klinect (2006)[4], flight crews who develop contingency management plans, such as proactively discussing strategies for anticipated threats, tend to have fewer mismanaged threats; crews that exhibit good monitoring and cross-checking usually commit fewer errors and have few mismanaged errors; and finally, crews that exhibit strong leadership, enquiry and workload management are typically observed to have fewer mismanaged errors and undesired aircraft states than other crews.

Many of the best practices advocated by crew resource management (CRM) can be considered TEM countermeasures.

Systemic Based Countermeasures

All countermeasures are flight crew actions. However, some countermeasures are based upon 'hard' resources. These are preventative systems, checks and procedures. They are *systemic–based countermeasures* (they are part of the total flight safety system) and can include:

- Airborne Collision Avoidance System (ACAS)
- Standard operating procedures
- Checklists
- Briefing
- Training, etc.

---

[3] https://skylibrarys.files.wordpress.com/2016/07/doc-9683-human-factor-training-manual.pdf

[4] Merritt, A. and Klinect, J. (2006). Defensive Flying for Pilots: An Introduction to Threat and Error Management. The Universty of Texas Human Factors Research Project, The LOSA Collaborative. See: https://www.skybrary.aero/bookshelf/ books/1982.pdf

Individual and Team Countermeasures

Other countermeasures are more directly related to the human contribution to the safety of flight operations. These are personal strategies and tactics, individual and team countermeasures that typically include canvassed skills, knowledge and attitudes developed by human performance training, most notably, by Crew Resource Management (CRM) training.

There are three categories of individual and team countermeasures:

- **Planning countermeasures**: essential for managing anticipated and unexpected threats;
- **Execution countermeasures**: essential for error detection and error response;
- **Review countermeasures**: essential for managing the changing conditions of a flight.

Examples of these are as follows:

Planning Countermeasures

SOP Briefing	The required briefing was interactive and operationally thorough	■ Concise, not rushed, and met SOP requirements ■ Bottom lines were established
Plans Stated	Operational plans and decisions were communicated and acknowledged	■ Shared understanding about plans - "Everybody on the same page"
Workload Assignment	Roles and responsibilities were defined for normal and non-normal situations	■ Workload assignments were communicated and acknowledged
Contingency Management	Crew members developed effective strategies to manage threats to safety	■ Threats and their consequences were anticipated ■ Used all available resources to manage threats

Execution Countermeasures

Monitor / Cross-check	Crew members actively monitored and cross-checked systems and other crew members	■ Aircraft position, settings, and crew actions were verified
Workload Management	Operational tasks were prioritized and properly managed to handle primary flight duties	■ Avoided task fixation ■ Did not allow work overload
Automation Management	Automation was properly managed to balance situational and/or workload requirements	■ Automation setup was briefed to other members ■ Effective recovery techniques from automation anomalies

Review Countermeasures

Evaluation/ Modification of Plans	Existing plans were reviewed and modified when necessary	■ Crew decisions and actions were openly analyzed to make sure the existing plan was the best plan
Inquiry	Crew members asked questions to investigate and/or clarify current plans of action	■ Crew members not afraid to express a lack of knowledge - "Nothing taken for granted" attitude
Assertiveness	Crew members stated critical information and/or solutions with appropriate persistence	■ Crew members spoke up without hesitation

Summary

- The threat and error management (TEM) approach has been developed based on the recognition that human error is a normal part of human behaviour and should be managed.
- TEM promotes a philosophy of anticipation of 'thinking ahead' in the constantly changing environment of flight operations.
- The three basic components of the TEM model are threats, errors and undesired aircraft states.
- Flight crews who develop strategies or countermeasures such as planning, execution and review/modify plans tend to have fewer mismanaged threats. They commit fewer errors, have fewer mismanaged errors and fewer undesired aircraft states than other crews.

Crew Resource Management

How crews work together in an aircraft has been referred to in many different ways, including Aircrew coordination, Cockpit Resource Management, Cockpit coordination, Cockpit Communication Management, Crew Air Management System, and Crew Resource Management, to name a few.

Each description above effectively describes the same principle, which, for convention, we will label in this course as Crew Resource Management or "*CRM*" for short.

CRM encompasses the operating procedures, words, phrases and actions that have been developed over time, allowing aircrews to have the same mental model for any given scenario. In having the same mental model, aircrews can communicate effectively with each other to achieve a safe outcome.

What is CRM

CRM is the effective management of all resources available to the flight crew to complete a safe and efficient flight.

Resources

The resources for CRM are principally management skills for **aircrew**, including:

- Communication
- Interpersonal skills
- Situational awareness
- Problem-solving
- Decision making
- Judgement
- Leadership
- Followership
- Stress management
- Threat and Error Management.

Other resources may include:

- Air Traffic Control
- Traffic in the vicinity
- Company operations
- Ground crew, and even
- Passengers.

Aircrew

It is essential to understand that the aircrew is not simply made up of the Captain and Co-pilot up front in the cockpit but can encompass all members of the aircraft crew who are on board or those other stakeholders that have a function and a role to play when interacting with the flight. Other stakeholders may include ATC, refuelers, ground support personnel, and other crews in another aircraft, to name a few.

Objectives of CRM

There are five (5) basic objectives in a CRM program that require all crew members to:

1. Establish and maintain team relationships
2. Conduct mission planning and rehearsal
3. Establish and maintain appropriate workloads
4. Exchange mission (sortie/task) information
5. Cross monitor each other's performance

Establish and Maintain Team Relationships

Free to communicate

Each member of a crew, regardless of their position, qualification, rank, role or responsibility, needs to be able to communicate openly and freely to work together to achieve the task safely.

In an aircraft, although the aircraft captain has the final say, a co-pilot, student, loadmaster, crew chief or other crewmembers should always be able to point out, discuss or mention information that may be important.

Example

For example, consider a helicopter about to lift off, and a crew member in the back notices a person approaching the helicopter from the rear. They should be able to speak up without any hesitation or fear of reprisal.

Team leadership

Part of making up a good team is having a Captain who will provide team leadership and foster an environment within the aircraft that allows crew communication.

Good team leaders foster a team; bad team leaders do not.

Video:

Watch the video of an old 1960s movie where John Wayne is flying as the co-pilot of a WWII aircraft.

This is a classic CRM video clip where the Captain demands the Flight Engineer prepare for a landing, but both the Co-pilot and the Flight Engineer disagree with that decision. This results in the Co-Pilot taking control and smacking his Captain around the head for not listening. Not a lot of team discussion here, just a lot of yelling and abuse.

Link: http://www.youtube.com/watch?v=ZnrTq9Y-uJY

This is also pretty good: https://www.youtube.com/watch?v=kgGxhHAKW9U

Aircrews are Teams

Lines of authority and responsibility	Aircrews are teams with a designated leader and clear lines of authority and responsibility.
Setting the tone	The aircraft Captain will set the tone for the crew and maintain the working environment.
Effective leaders	Effective leaders use their authority but do not operate without the participation of other crew members.

Resolving disagreements	When crew members disagree on a course of action, they must be effective in resolving the disagreement.
Methods to resolve disagreements	Specific methods to achieve this may include: ■ The aircraft Captain actively establishes an open climate where crew members freely talk and ask questions. ■ Crew members value each other for their expertise and judgement. They do not allow differences in culture, background, age and experience to influence their willingness to speak up. ■ Alternative viewpoints are a normal and occasional part of crew interaction. Crew members handle disagreements in a professional manner, avoiding personal attacks or defensive posturing. ■ The aircraft captain actively monitors the attitudes of crew members and offers feedback when necessary. Each crew member displays the proper concern for balancing safety with task accomplishment.

Cockpit Gradient

Leaders and Followers

Like in any team, there must be a leader in an aircraft, and there must be followers.

The leader will have the ultimate responsibility for the overall management of the task. However, supporting that leader is a second-in-command, followed by the remaining team members, who each have a role to play and may be responsible for an area of importance.

> **Example**
>
> Consider a football team (let's use rugby as the example)
>
> The leader is the Captain, and the second leader is the Vice-Captain, but underneath them will be other leaders responsible for their specialised areas in the team. In this case, there will be a leader for the forwards, a leader for the backs, a leader for the scrum, a leader for the lineout, etc.

---

[5] Adidas All Blacks by Natural Heart / CC by-SA 2.0 / https://www.flickr.com/photos/30291646@N03/6150517434 -

Authority Gradient

These varying levels of leadership are referred to as the "Authority Gradient".

Each person will have specific levels of authority based on their position within the team and will be empowered to make certain decisions based on rules that have been determined by the Coach (Company or Military Unit).

Figure 1   Authority Gradient

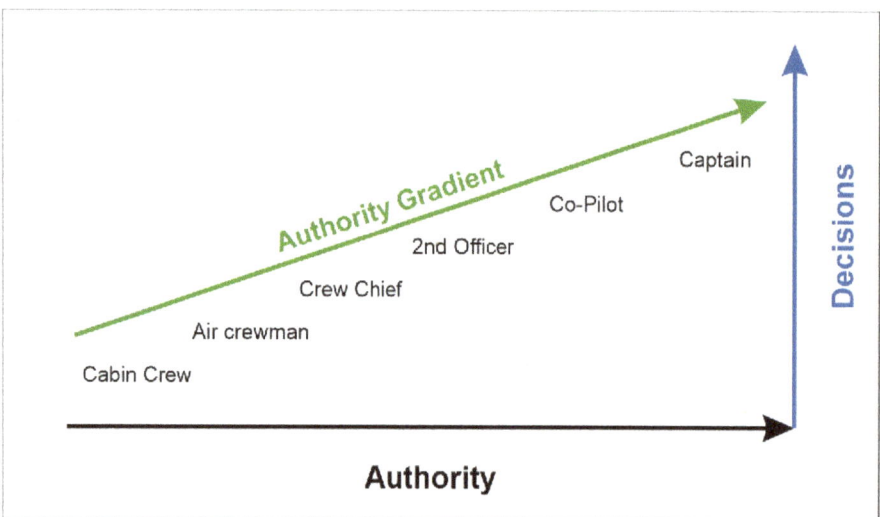

This authority may be:

- Explicit, where the leadership is defined and written down in rules and procedures, or
- Implied, where the leadership is defined by social convention, culture and expectation and may not be written down.

Cockpit Gradient

In aviation, the Authority Gradient is referred to as the "*Cockpit Authority Gradient*" or just *"Cockpit Gradient"* for short because it concerns the pilots in the cockpit.

A cockpit authority gradient should allow for teamwork, communication and problem solving between the pilots and crew while maintaining a clear command structure.

The challenge for CRM is generating and maintaining a gradient that allows for authority to be maintained while also allowing for open and constructive communication and teamwork.

Obstructions

Sometimes obstructions appear that break down communication, and the crew stop working as a team.

This can happen for many reasons, including:

- **Culture**
  A flight crew's ethnic culture can significantly affect cockpit dynamics. Pilots are required to put their culture aside and operate the aircraft professionally in accordance with the CRM Standard Operation Procedures (SOPs). The two most common communication breakdowns due to culture are;
  - A junior pilot who is culturally more important than the experienced pilot, to the point where the experienced pilot ceases to be PIC (for example, consider a Prince or Sheik or similar who is also a pilot flying with a new crew) and
  - An experienced senior Captain where the Co-Pilot is afraid to speak up or advise the senior pilot for fear of embarrassing the Captain.
- One of the other crew members lower down in the gradient line asserts themselves as the key decision-maker
- The Captain does not listen to the advice or use the other crew members, making them feel alienated
- A captain is directive and authoritarian
- Other crew members lack the confidence to engage with the Captain at the right level
- The Captain lacks the confidence to work with other crew members at the right level.

Adverse Authority Gradient

When the authority gradient is unbalanced, it is referred to as an 'adverse authority gradient'. Something has happened that is preventing the crew from working together.

The evidence of an adverse authority gradient is often shown in the results of accident investigations where:

- Co-pilots were afraid to point-out errors
- Captains disregarded the advice of another crew member
- Crew members talked each other into trouble because nobody was acting like a leader

Figure 2   Example of an Adverse Authority Gradient

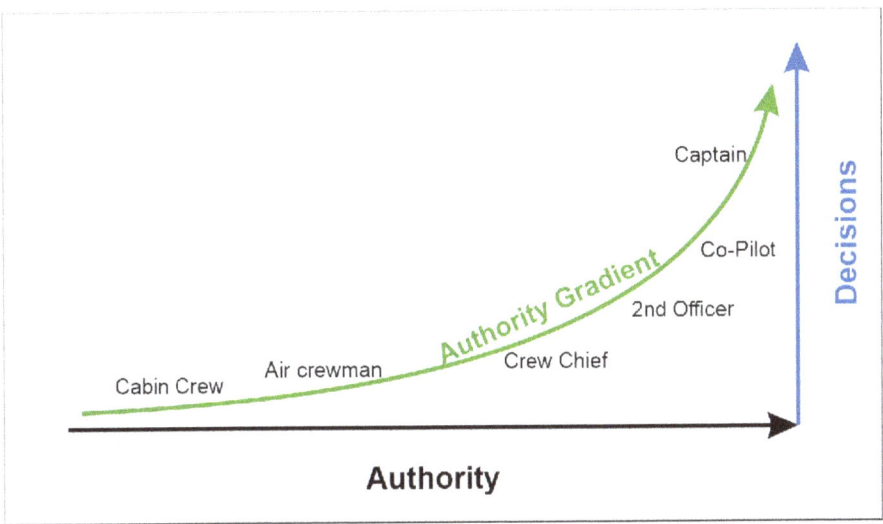

Much of the CRM training is based on understanding how teams work together. It is the role of a Captain to lead by example, and it is the role of a Co-Pilot to be a good follower. If a Captain spends too much time emphasising that he is the boss, an adverse cockpit gradient may result, and a Co-Pilot may feel afraid to speak up. This can be a challenge to get right, and the crew must be aware of any adverse cockpit authority gradient.

Shallow Authority Gradient

During normal Multi-Crew operations, the aim is to achieve a shallow authority gradient. The Captain knows that he or she is in ultimate command, and the Co-Pilot is aware that their role is to support the Captain, but this is done in a team environment, not an authoritarian environment.

Although the Captain has the ultimate decision-making ability, this privilege should only be applied after consulting with the team and assimilating all the facts to make a decision. Sometimes the Captain will let the team make some decisions within their level of authority on their own because they are trusted. At other times the Captain may have to make quick decisions that the team will just have to follow.

Figure 3   Example of a Shallower Authority Gradient

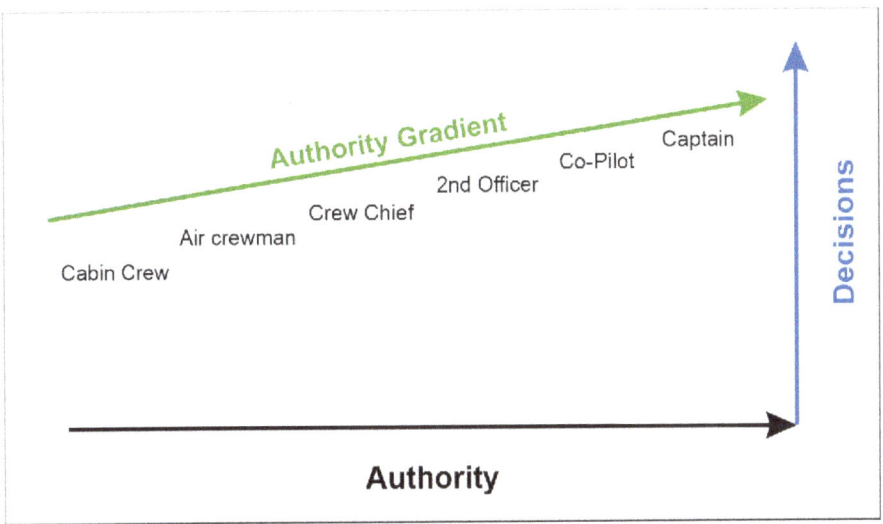

Executive Decision

A decision that the Captain *'just makes'* regardless of the crew's input is known as an ***"Executive Decision"***.

Sometimes, especially in emergency or time-critical situations, the Captain will exercise the Executive Decision rights and not consult the team but simply go ahead with a determined course of action, and the crew will have to support the Captain in the decision.

During flight operations, the goal is to work together at a level where the requirement for Executive Decision making is minimised, and the crew can problem solve through cooperation and application of sound CRM. This, however, takes time.

Followership

Ensuring a working authority gradient is not just the responsibility of the leader. The follower must also be able to understand how to work on maintaining a positive gradient and how to 'step up' to being a good follower and working on the authority gradient, rather than always deferring to and being a servant to the leader.

Figure 4   Example of a Complementary Followership – Leadership Gradient

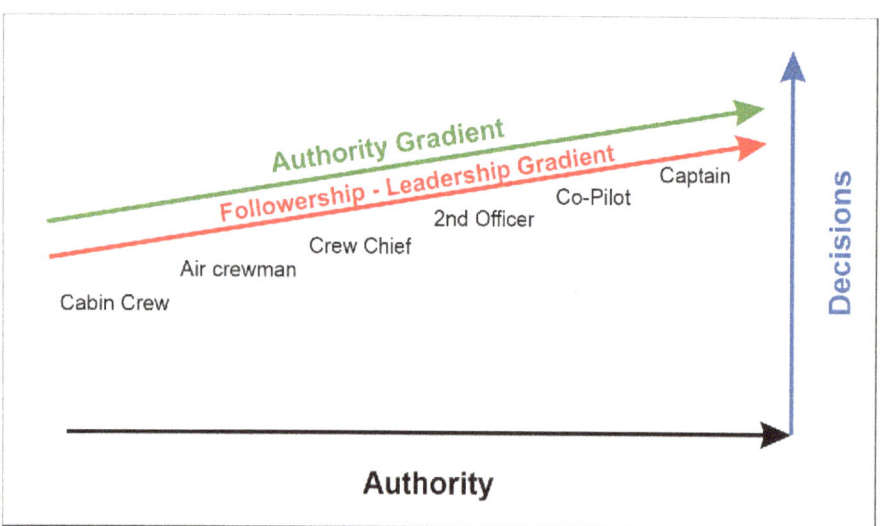

Building and maintaining a working authority gradient is helped through awareness, CRM training, consistent application of standards and a supportive organisational policy. This combination provides a framework within which leaders and followers can work together to achieve their goals and maximise their ability to communicate and safely operate the aircraft together.

Ego States

Ego States

In the 1950s, Dr Eric Berne created the concept of Ego States. An ego state is a consistent pattern of feeling and experience directly related to a corresponding pattern of behaviour. Many people (including pilots) subconsciously adopt different ego states and display that behaviour depending on the immediate physical and social setting in which people live or in which something happens or develops:

Dr Berne defined three (3) ego states that can be confirmed by observable behaviour. They are the:

- Parent ego state
- Adult ego state
- Child ego state

Parent ego state

The **parent** ego state encompasses the external events that were imposed on a person in the first five years of their life. These are constructs or boundaries that are imposed on the child.

For example:

A parent will say things like "Don't talk to strangers", "Always hold a grown-up's hand when you cross the road", or "Don't touch a hot stove."

The parent ego state will mean the person displays behaviour that;

- Scolds
- Points Fingers
- Lectures on rights and wrongs
- Always corrects

Adult ego state

The **adult** ego state evaluates what is really going on and makes independent decisions about the world. This ego state begins forming as soon as we gain the ability to control aspects of our environment. It allows a person to compare what they are told about the world with what they feel and experience.

For example:

The adult is told by the parent not to touch a hot stove and recognizes the child's fear of being burned is reasonable. Therefore, the adult determines to use caution when it is necessary to use a hot stove.

The adult ego state will mean a person displays behaviour that;

- Is factual and rational
- Makes decisions
- Listens
- Suggests alternatives
- Rationalises

Child ego state

The **child** ego state contains the feelings and emotions related to the external events that were imposed on a person in the first five years of life. These feelings or emotions are replayed in the person's mind when the corresponding external event is recalled.

For example:

A child "would be nervous if being approached by a stranger,"' "Feels safe when holding someone's hand,"' or "Is scared of being burned."

The child ego state will mean a person displays behaviour that;

- Expresses feelings
- Whines, sulks and has tantrums
- Expresses joy

Summary

Pilots

When operating in a multi-crew environment, pilots are clearly expected to behave like Adults. That is to be factual, rational, make decisions, listen, make suggestions and rationalise. However, when put under pressure or in the right (or wrong) situation, a person can fall into one of the other ego states and act like a parent or a child.

These can have an effect on flight-deck dynamics and relationships. An adult subjected to Parent-like behaviour can subconsciously move into the childlike state without realising it. This is destructive for cockpit relationships and crew co-operation and is something to be mindful of.

For example:

It could be easy for a Captain to display a Parent ego state and start pointing fingers, lecturing on the rights and wrongs on a particular point and always correct.

Just as easily, the Co-Pilot could then revert to a Child ego state and respond with emotion, whine, and sulk or throw a tantrum.

Verbal Communication

Ways we communicate

During day-to-day conversation, communication does not just happen verbally; we also get people's attention and communicate by using body language; this may include:

- Making eye contact
- A light touch
- An exclamation
- A hand gesture
- The way we stand (our posture)

During flight operations, these attention-getting cues may not be available or difficult to properly interpret, giving a much heavier reliance on the spoken word (verbal communication).

---

6 Geralty, (2022), https://pixabay.com/en/men-silhouette-tie-businessmen-102441

7 Tiger ,(2022), https://www.airbushelicopterscom/website/en/ref/Tiger_51.html

What you say is what you hear

Because verbal communication is now the most important tool the pilots have to communicate, it is important that what you say is what you mean, as that is what the other crewmember will hear and react to. Getting that communication wrong can be the beginning of an undesired aircraft state.

For flight operations, procedures and standards are needed to structure this verbal communication:

- The use of standard words and phrases ensures that communications have precise and clear meaning.
- Acknowledgement ensures that the message has been heard and understood.
- The readback introduces redundancy and confirms that the information received is correct.
- Using direct language prevents misinterpretation.
- A statement of intent makes a course of action clear and removes assumptions prior to actually commencing the action.

These standard words, phrases and procedures are usually found in Company or Military Unit **S**tandard **O**perating **P**rocedures (**SOP**s).

Saying and hearing the right things requires a pilot to have:

- Good listening skills
- Positive communication skills
- Being assertive, not passive
- Able to monitor and give feedback (appraisal)

Good listening

Listening is defined as *"receiving language through the ears, identifying the sounds of speech and processing them into words and sentences"*.

It is important to remember there is a difference between hearing and listening.

Hearing is the physical process of the ear receiving noise.

Listening means that the crewmember has received the noise and then used their brain to interpret and understand what the noise was in accordance with the definition above.

Based on this interpretation, the crewmember will give a response either by responding verbally or commencing an action. Listening is, therefore, a process where the receiver hears a noise, focuses on the message, interprets it, then analyses it before making a response and then remembering it as an experience for next time.

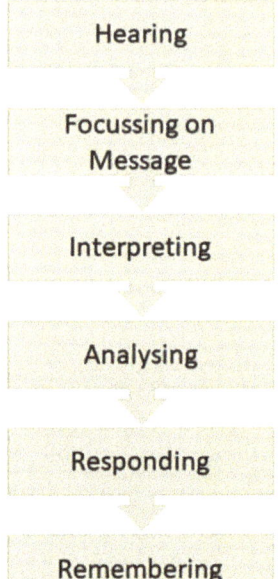

Active Listening

Communication Breakdown

There are many areas where the communication between crew members can break down.

The person speaking may not use the right words or phrases; the person hearing may not interpret those words correctly or misunderstand what was being said.

Failure to process and understand information can cause problems and conflicts such as:

- The wrong message leading to the wrong response
- Wasted time
- Frustration
- Misunderstanding and confusion
- Lack of confidence on the part of the speaker
- Uncertainty on the part of the receiver

In order to reduce these issues, it is critical in a team environment that the crew utilises Active Listening techniques.

Active listening

Active listening is the deliberate act of mindfully hearing and attempting to comprehend the meaning of words spoken by another in a conversation.

In other words, you are paying attention and are actively part of the conversation.

Active listening is an important skill that a pilot in a team environment needs to cultivate. It will involve making sounds that indicate attentiveness and the listener giving feedback in the form of acknowledgements and readbacks of what has been said by the other party for their confirmation.

Stress and Conflict

Causes of stress

We are subjected to stressors throughout our everyday lives. During our early flight training and Human Factors lessons, we learn the importance of identifying and managing stress in our lives to ensure that we don't take dangerous distractions flying with us.

When operating in a Multi-crew environment, you also have to identify and understand what may be causing stress to your colleagues or the crew.

Think about the helicopter cockpit. There are many causes of stress:

Physical

- Environment
- Noise
- Vibration
- Temperature
- Ergonomics
- Weather

Type of Operations

- Medivac
- SAR
- Fire

Think about your crew. There we can also find causes of stress:

Physical

- Fatigue
- Lack of fitness
- Hunger

Physiological

- Workload
- Tests
- Checks
- Career
- Personal life

Managing stress and conflict

In order to reach 'peak performance' all crew members should consider the needs of the rest of the crew.

Maslow's hierarchy of needs is presented in many human factors texts as an illustration of the importance of aircrew in understanding the effects that external and internal stressors have on their performance. In terms of multi-crew working, awareness of the effects that the actions of other crew members can have on individual performance is also important.

Some of the aspects of Maslow relevant to multi-crew operations may not be immediately apparent. A major tool for reducing stress and conflict in a cockpit is being aware of the possibility and consequences of placing individuals in positions that make them uncomfortable, and ensuring that your team feels empowered to raise suggestions or concerns without fear of reprisal.

Figure 5   Maslow's Hirearchy of Needs

Let's consider some of the ways in which actions of other crew members can affect individual performance:

Creating a positive environment

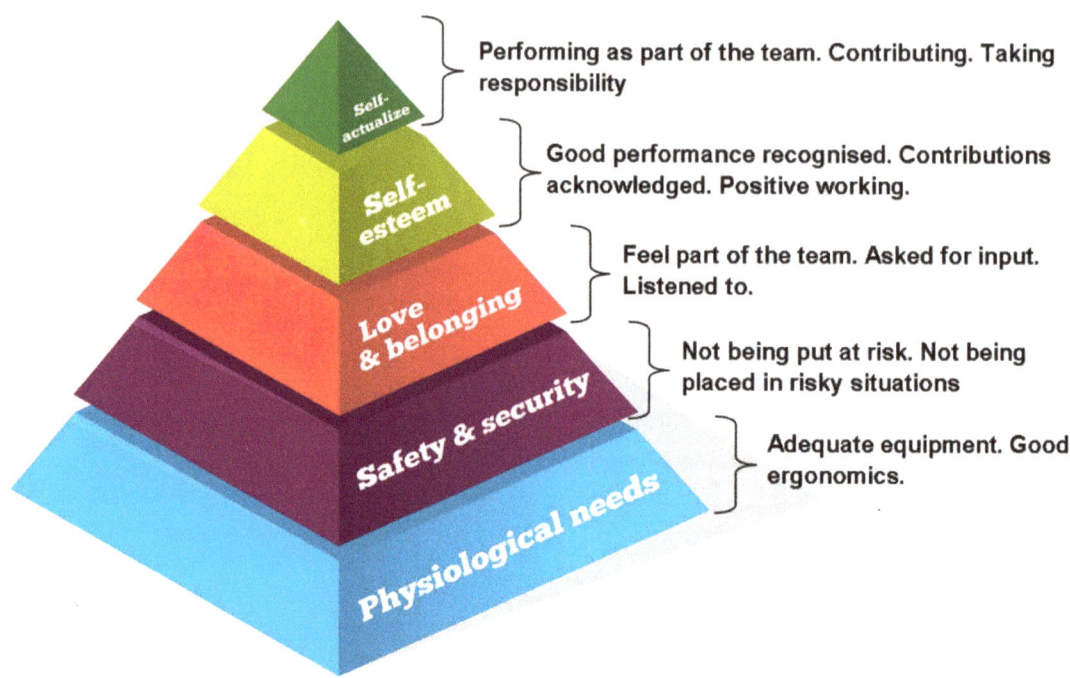

Safety and Security is an important area to understand in the context of Multi-Crew operations. It is obvious that inclusion in a team and positive working practices improve performance. In terms of safety and security, try to consider non-physical risks. The physical safety of an aircraft and crew are always the primary concern for pilots, but how do safety and security translate to individual performance in a multi-crew environment?

Think about an adverse authority gradient or a Pilot in Command (PIC) who is taking risky courses of action that make the Second in Command (SIC) feel uncomfortable (in terms of rule-breaking, not physical safety). Is that PIC affecting the safety and security of the SIC by generating an unknown risk of conflict or consequence when the SIC speaks up? Could this behaviour cause the SIC to feel pressure on their security in terms of professional reputation and future repercussions?

In a crew environment, communication is king. Taking opportunities from the pre-flight briefing through to the end of the debrief and ensuring an open, sharing environment is essential to reducing conflict by ensuring that problems are identified and managed early on.

- Talk to each other
- Discuss weaknesses
- Share experiences
- Acknowledge causes of external stress
- Be supportive and constructive
- Assist in managing workloads
- Motivate and support

Team Communication

In order to achieve effective team communication, all members of the crew are required to:

1. Communicate in the same language
2. Communicate positively
3. Communicate actively
4. Direct assistance
5. Announce actions
6. Offer assistance
7. Acknowledge actions

8. Be explicit
9. Provide aircraft control and obstacle advisories
10. Co-ordinate action sequence and timing

1. Communicate in the Same Language

English is the common language used in aviation. To avoid confusion, non-native English speakers need to develop and improve their English speaking and listening skills. Using standard phrases and avoiding the use of slang, casual or conversational English can prevent confusion between the speaker and listener.

Video:

Link: http://www.youtube.com/watch?v=hXWfgRK0XcA&feature=related

Link: https://www.youtube.com/watch?v=hzqdDoe8FoM

2. Communicate Positively

Good cockpit teamwork requires positive communication among crew members. Positive communication should consider:

1. The type of language used, and
2. The way the words are delivered and received.

Type of language used

Positive communication in the style of language used

It is important for crew relationships that mutual respect and good professional attitudes exist, rather than autocratic, directive leadership.

For example, consider a Flying Pilot not maintaining altitude. The Pilot monitoring simply has to say the word "Altitude", at which point the Flying Pilot should acknowledge and correct the altitude. If the Flying Pilot does not respond, the Pilot Monitoring may follow up with "the aircraft is descending; we need to maintain 1000 feet". This communication style is better than the Pilot Monitoring saying, "You are not maintaining your height; fix it up".

Crews need to consider how others will respond to words used, which can have cultural implications.

Way the words are delivered

Positive communication in the way the words are delivered and received

Communication is positive when the sender directs, announces, requests, or offers information; the receiver acknowledges the information; the sender confirms the information, based on the receiver's acknowledgment or action.

The receiver must anticipate what the sender says or wants and listen carefully. Either crew member must have no doubt about what is said or meant before taking action. This is positive communication.

3. Communicate Accurately

How we communicate

Working in aviation we communicate using radios or intercoms. This can create challenges and barriers to effective communications as we cannot see facial or physical cues.

In day-to-day life, people rely on non-verbal communication:

 **Video:** http://www.maximumadvantage.com/nonverbal-communication/non-verbal-communication-demonstration.html[8]

The words we use in day-to-day communication are not the only way that we communicate.

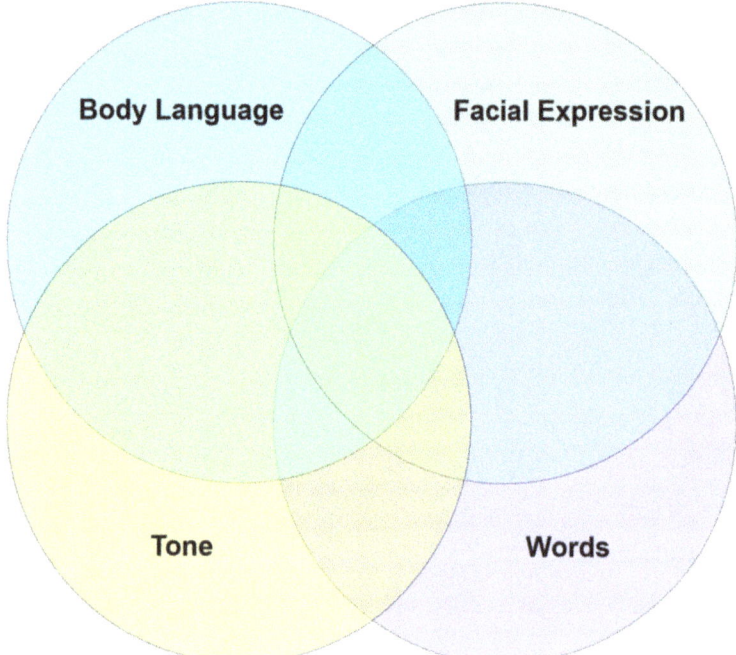

Body language, tone, and facial expressions are important to get our message across when we speak. Particularly in environments where pressure or authority is present, body language, tone and facial expressions are essential to ensure that our mood, motives and emotions are understood.

When we fly an aircraft, we lose much of this ability. We must rely only on the words we use.

Even tone can be problematic if it does not come with re-enforcement from body language. Imagine that you thought you heard in somebody's voice that they were irritated. Do they have their arms crossed? What is their facial expression? How do you know if they are irritated or not?

We also build in additional pressures, such as the need for brevity and the use of standard words and phrases during radio communications. These challenges can be made even more severe when we work with people from different cultures, or who are non-native speakers.

---

[8] Endress, Paul (n.d.), Non-Verbal Communication Demonstration from Maximum advantage, Psychology Applied to Life, accessed online 19 May 2022, http://www.maximumadvantage.com/nonverbal-communication/non-verbal-communication-demonstration.html

9 By U.S. Navy photo by Mass Communication Specialist 2nd Class Aaron Burden [Public domain], via Wikimedia Commons / https://commons.wikimedia.org/wiki/File%3AUS_Navy_061017-N-7130B-030_An_instructor_pilot_is_joined_by_his_student_in_the_cockpit_of_a_T-45A_Goshawk_on_the_flight_deck_aboard_the_Nimitz-class_aircraft_carrier_USS_Ronald_Reagan_(CVN_76).jpg

10 U.S. Air Force photo by Staff Sgt. Jacob Morgan) / https://media.defense.gov/2013/Nov/22/2000893886/-1/-1/0/131116-F-AB304-067.JPG

Multi-Crew Cooperation *for Helicopter Pilots*

Tools for effective verbal communication

- Avoid shortcuts that you might use in day-to-day communication, like sarcasm or humour.
- Don't use slang.
- Try not to rely on tone. If you have a problem, make a positive statement to begin to resolve it.
- If brief and standard phrases are failing, don't persevere with being misunderstood. Revert to plain English to resolve your problem.
- Try to work with the same people on the same job. As you get to know each other's manner, communication should improve.
- Use appropriate words like 'please' and 'thanks' to ensure that verbal transactions are effectively concluded.
- Don't take offence to something that you think sounds harsh or abrasive. If required, clarify a situation.
- Do address behaviours directly if you believe they are causing a CRM issue. <u>BUT</u> try to wait for the debrief rather than in-flight (unless the behaviour causes an immediate flight safety concern). Remember, your attempts at communicating without visual cues may also be unsuccessful!

Example

Sarah is conducting aerial fire fighting operations. She found one ground controller particularly easy to work with; they shared mental processes and were able to work efficiently to gain common situational awareness. When she returned to base, Sarah called the regional firefighting centre to let them know that the ground controller did a great job and that she found him easy to work with.

The firefighting centre usually rotated personnel through the ground controller role, but they made the decision to maintain the same person in the position for the duration of the operation. This meant that the operation proceeded smoothly, safely and efficiently.

4. Direct Assistance

Direct or ask for assistance

Direct assistance is when a crew member will **direct or ask for assistance** when the task cannot be completed by the crew member on their own. It may be something important or unimportant. The point here is that assistance is required, and the crew member needs to ask for or direct another crew member to do or assist in the task. This assistance can be for controlling the aircraft, maintaining position or maintaining the required clearances from obstacles. It may be to direct or ask for assistance when troubleshooting aircraft systems or conducting normal checklists.

In a crewed environment, the purpose of the other pilot or crew member is to *share* the operating load to ensure that together all crewmembers have ample spare capacity.

Example

Consider an aircraft operating in bad weather. The Pilot Flying (PF) may have his hands busy flying the aircraft accurately, especially when in instrument meteorological conditions (IMC). It might be usual for the PF to select autopilot modes, but why not ask the Pilot Monitoring (PM) to engage the autopilot if that would result in the smoothest flight. This utilises the PM's spare capacity and allows the PF's hands to remain on the controls.

5. Announce Actions

To ensure effective and well-coordinated actions in the aircraft, all crew members must be aware of the expected movements and unexpected individual actions. Each crew member will announce any actions that affect the activities of the other crew members.

Example

A helicopter is conducting fire-fighting operations, and the FP uses a GPS waypoint to judge his distance from the drop point. While the FP is busy in the hover, ATC asks for a position report relative to a nearby airfield, so the PM enters a new waypoint into the GPS and passes the distance information on to ATC.

The PM doesn't state to the PF that the GPS has been adjusted and because the PF was concentrating on a critical manoeuvre, the FP doesn't notice the change. Once the task is complete, the PF maintains control but becomes spatially disoriented when his mental picture doesn't match the information on his flight display as the GPS is no longer referencing the drop point.

6. Offer Assistance

A crew member will provide assistance or information that has been requested. He will also offer assistance when he sees that another crew member needs help.

Example

The PM notices the PF searching around the flight deck with his eyes and realizes that the PF is distracted. He asks if everything is OK, and the PF says that he's lost his pen. The PM offers to take control of the helicopter and scan duties while the PF conducts a more thorough search.

7. Acknowledge Actions

Communications in the aircraft must include supportive feedback to ensure that crew members correctly understand announcements or directives.

Example

If a crew member needs to open a door, he should first announce that he is going to open the door. He should not open the door until all other crew members have acknowledged this.

8. Be Explicit

Clear terms and phrases

Crew members should use clear terms and phrases and positively acknowledge critical information.

Avoid multiple meanings

They must avoid using terms that have multiple meanings, such as;

"*Right*"

Does that mean "turn right" or "yes, you are right", or I am acknowledging you"

"*Back up*"

Does that mean "go backwards" or "say again what you just said" or "go back up" or "increase altitude"

"*I have it.*"

Does that mean "I have control", "I have the item you were looking for", or "I know the answer"

Avoid indefinite modifiers

Crew members must also avoid using indefinite modifiers such as, "Do you see that tree?" or "You are coming in a little fast". An indefinite modifier means that you cannot identify exactly what the other person is referring to. Which tree? There are 50 in front of me. How fast? 5 kt, 10 kt, 100 kt? Crews need to be very specific to avoid confusion.

9. Provide Aircraft Control and Obstacle Advisories

Although the pilot is responsible for aircraft control, the other crew members may need to provide aircraft control information regarding airspeed, altitude, or obstacle avoidance. This will be part of their normal responsibilities, and crews would have been briefed before a flight as to what those are. In these circumstances, the PF should not have to ask for assistance, but it should be freely given as part of that crew member's core responsibility. This is where crews that work together often develop trust and a known working environment which leads to greater efficiencies.

10. Co-ordinate Action Sequence and Timing

Proper sequencing and timing ensure that the actions of one crew member will mesh with the actions of the other crew members.

Example

Consider an NVG mission. The helicopter lifts off the ground. The PF will commence the hover checks by stating, "Controls feel normal, C of G feels normal" then, without any request or delay, the PM will then complete the check by announcing, "warning lights are out, T'S and P's are in the green, RPM top of the green, power required is 75% Cat 4 power and pedal position noted".

This shows a seamless work environment with CRM working as it should as the PF while on NVG is flying the aircraft and looking outside, the PM has the eyes inside duties.

Practice Good Intercom Discipline

The nature of conducting complex tasks in a noisy helicopter environment means that it may take a moment for a pilot or crew member to realize that they are being addressed. Therefore, when addressing a colleague on the intercom in the aircraft, a pilot or crew member should first address him or her by their Executive Role before stating the issue.

In general, it works best to use formal titles to ensure that no confusion exists. Company policies may vary, but usually, the pilot in command (PIC) is addressed as "Captain", while the second in command (SIC) is addressed as "Co-pilot". If addressing crewmembers in the back of the helicopter, this is better done by referring to either their seating position or role.

---

11 Photo: LA(Phot) Stuart Hill/MOD [OGL (http://www.nationalarchives.gov.uk/doc/open-government-licence/version/1/)], via Wikimedia Commons / https://commons.wikimedia.org/wiki/File%3AAircrew_Onboard_Royal_Navy_Merlin_Helicopter_MOD_45150943.jpg

> **Example**

If the Captain wanted to speak to the crewman seated in the back left of the helicopter to ask if the area was clear for a landing, the communication may go as follows;

Captain: "Back left, confirm the area is clear."

Crewmember "Back left is clear."

Conduct Mission Planning and Rehearsal

Introduction

Mission planning and rehearsal are where each member of the crew, together, is able to explore all aspects of the mission, task or sortie. This will require the analysis and rehearsal of each part of the task to identify potential difficulties and efficiencies within the guidelines given for the task. In aircraft, this directly relates to the flight planning stages of the flight.

> **Example**

Consider the planning of an NVG sortie. Each crew member should consult with each other on the weather, the LSALT, the route, obstacles, wires, etc. Each may bring new information and a new way of thinking to each new piece of information.

Planning

Tasks include planning for VFR, NVFR (NUA), IFR or NVG. Planning for the type of mission may include training, troop incursion or extraction, reconnaissance, transport, etc.

Crew responsibilities

Planning will also include assigning crew member responsibilities and conducting all required briefings and readbacks.

---

12 By U.S. Navy photo by Photographer's Mate 2nd Class Michael Sandberg. [Public domain], via Wikimedia Commons / https://commons.wikimedia.org/wiki/File%3AUS_Navy_021217-N-4374S-
019_Aircrew_Survival_Equipmentman_1st_Class_David_Cummings%2C_assigned_to_the_Vanguards_of_Helicopter_Mine_Countermeasure_Squadron_Fourteen_(HM-14).jpg

Pre-mission rehearsals

Pre-mission rehearsal involves the crew collectively visualising and discussing expected and potentially unexpected events for the entire sortie. Through this process, all crew members think through contingencies and actions for complex segments or unusual events associated with the mission and develop strategies to cope with contingencies.

Establish and Maintain Appropriate Workloads

Establishing and maintaining appropriate workloads involves giving each crew member their specific duties and responsibilities for the task, with backup tasking discussed. If a crew member becomes busy or needs to concentrate on a critical task, some of their responsibilities may then be shared by other crew members.

Example

Consider in an aircraft the requirement to maintain an effective lookout. If a pilot is looking inside the cockpit and concentrating on the aircraft systems, another crew member will have to take up the scan.

Announcing actions

Shared situational awareness is important when operating as part of a crew. If one crew member activates a service or changes a frequency, then they need to let the other crew members know. Make communicating what you are doing part of the normal flow of operating. In critical sorties, such as NVG, the crew cannot actually see each other. In these circumstances, it becomes critical that each crew member announces their actions so that all crew members are aware of what the other is doing.

Example

The PM has to work the radios, so will announce "eyes inside front left". The FP will then reply with "taking up the scan".

High workload

When the workload is high, such as when low flying, taking off, and landing, the pilots have to decide

Example

Consider a helicopter on approach to land, and the crew member in the back starts asking the aircraft captain about a passenger's health. Is it more important to look after the passenger or safely land the aircraft?

The following video sets this same scenario up in a fixed wing. While watching I want you to think what could have been done differently and this will be discussed after.

Link: https://www.youtube.com/watch?v=8ZIHGQT4X9w

Exchange Mission (Sortie/Task) Information

Standard words and phrases

When exchanging mission information, using standard words, phrases and methodologies become increasingly important. So that whatever is said is understood, giving all the crew the same mental picture (also referred to as the mental model) of what is happening or about to happen.

This requires practice, good coordination and trust within the crew.

> **Example**
>
> Consider an aircraft about to conduct a right turn. The crew member that can see will clear the turn and use standard words such as "clear left, ahead and above" so that the other crew know that part of the sky has been cleared before the turn.

Statements and directives are clear, timely, relevant, complete, and verified.

This quality refers to the completeness, timeliness, and quality of information transfer. It includes the crew's use of standard terminology and feedback techniques to verify information transfer. Emphasis is on the quality of instructions and statements associated with navigation, obstacle clearance, and instrument readouts. Specific methods used include:

- Crew members consistently make the required callouts. Their statements and directives are always timely.
- Crew members use standard terminology in all communications. Their statements and directives are clear and concise.
- Crew members actively seek feedback when they do not receive an acknowledgment from another crew member. They always acknowledge understanding of intent and request clarification when necessary.

Sortie situational awareness is maintained.

This quality considers the extent to which crew members keep each other informed about the status of the aircraft and the sortie. Information reporting helps the aircrew maintain a high level of situational awareness. The information reported includes aircraft position and orientation, equipment and personnel status, environmental conditions, and changes to task objectives. Awareness of the situation by the entire crew is essential to safe flight and effective crew performance. Specific methods used include:

- Crew members routinely update each other and highlight and acknowledge changes. They take personal responsibility for scanning the entire flight environment, considering their assigned workload and areas of scanning.
- Crew members actively discuss conditions and situations that can compromise situational awareness. These include, but are not limited to, stress, boredom, fatigue, and anger.

Decisions and actions are communicated and acknowledged.

This quality addresses the extent to which crew members are kept informed of decisions made and actions taken by other crew members. Crew members should respond verbally or by appropriately adjusting their behaviours, actions, or control inputs to clearly indicate that they understand when a decision has been made and what it is. Failure to do so may confuse crew members and lead to uncoordinated operations. Specific methods include:

- Crew members announce decisions and actions, stating their rationale and intentions as time permits. The aircraft captain verbally coordinates the transfer of or inputs to controls before action.
- Crew members always acknowledge announced decisions or actions and provide feedback on how these decisions or actions will affect other crew tasks. If necessary, they promptly request clarification of decisions or actions.

Supporting information and actions are sought from the crew.

This quality addresses the extent to which supporting information and actions are sought from the crew by another crew member, usually the aircraft captain. Crew members should feel free to raise questions during the flight regarding plans, revisions to plans, actions to be taken, and the status of key sortie information. Specific methods include:

- The aircraft captain encourages crew members to raise issues or offer information about safety or the sortie. Crew members anticipate impending decisions and actions and offer information as appropriate.
- Crew members always request assistance from others before they become overloaded with tasks or before they must divert their attention from a critical task.

Consider working through a formal process to determine a sound course of action for complex problems. This allows the PIC to manage the decision-making process and allows all crew members to have input and take ownership of the final decision. See Phraseology for more information.

Unexpected events are managed effectively

This quality addresses the crew's performance under unusual circumstances that may involve high-stress levels. Both the technical and managerial aspects of coping with the situation are important. Specific methods include:

- Crew actions reflect extensive rehearsal of emergency procedures in prior training and pre-mission planning and rehearsal. Crew members coordinate their actions and exchange information with minimal verbal direction from the aircraft captain. They respond to the unexpected event in a composed, professional manner.
- Each crew member appropriately or voluntarily adjusts individual workload and task priorities with minimal verbal direction from the aircraft captain. The aircraft captain ensures that each crew member is used effectively when responding to an emergency and that the workload is efficiently distributed.
- Remember the importance of standard operating procedures (SOPs). A well-handled emergency invariable results from well-handled initial actions and SOPs. If you begin with actions that the other pilot is not expecting, capacity and situational awareness will be lost.

Cross Monitor Performance

Cross monitoring each other's performance is where each crew member will monitor the words and actions of each of the other crew members, and if an error or exclusion is made, one of the other crew members will speak up. In an aircraft, this is critical so that each other's actions and decisions are monitored to reduce the likelihood of errors impacting mission performance and safety.

> **Example**
>
> Consider an FP maintaining straight and level at 1000 feet at a cruise power of 75% torque. Due to a distraction, he allows the aircraft to commence a descent, and the power reduces to 65%. The PM, who is monitoring the PF's performance, will speak up and announce "Check Altitude". This will prompt the PF to correct the problem.

Advocacy and assertion are practised.

This quality concerns how crew members are proactive in advocating a course of action they consider best, even when others may disagree. Specific methods include:

- While maintaining a professional atmosphere, crew members state the rationale for their recommended plans and courses of action when time permits. They request feedback to ensure others have correctly understood their statements or rationale. Time permitting, other crew members practice good listening habits; they wait for the rationale before commenting on the recommended plans or courses of action. It is important that all crew members respect the words of the person talking and do not talk over or interrupt.
- The aircraft captain actively promotes objectivity in the cockpit by encouraging other crew members to speak up despite their rank or experience. Junior crew members do not hesitate to speak up when they disagree with senior members; they understand that more experienced aviators can sometimes make errors or lose situational awareness. Every member of the crew displays a sense of responsibility for adhering to flight regulations, operating procedures, and safety standards.

Crew-level post-sortie reviews are conducted.

This quality addresses the extent to which crew members review and critique their actions during or after a sortie segment, during periods of low workload, or during the sortie debriefing. Specific methods include

- The crew critiques major decisions and actions. They identify options and factors that should have been discussed and outline ways to improve crew performance in future sorties.
- The critique of crew decisions and actions is professional. "Finger-pointing" is avoided; the emphasis is on education and improvement of crew performance, not necessarily whose fault it is.
- **Lead by example;** *the standard that you walk by is the standard that you accept.* Credibility and integrity are key traits of any professional pilot. Be honest and open. If you felt that there were areas where your performance, or the crew's, could be improved, then bring it up and state what you could do about it. You won't be the only person who spotted the problem, but you might be the only one who wants to be part of the solution.
- Be willing to participate in your organisation's safety reporting system. Let others learn from issues that you faced. If during the debrief you identify that an aspect of the sortie would benefit from a report, make a team decision to file one.

Watch video Captain losing situational awareness:

Link: https://www.youtube.com/watch?v=rAstLZHjOi0

CRM for the Single Pilot

It is often asked, "What is the point of a CRM course for a single pilot?" With only one pilot on board and no crew, this is a valid question.

Checklists

The single-pilot does have another crew member on board – he is called "the checklist".

CRM for the single pilot

Using the appropriate checklists, applying Company procedures as stated in the Operations Manual, using Standard Operating Procedures (SOPs) provided by a contracting client, and even talking aloud to yourself and asking questions are all part of CRM for the single pilot.

Remember the importance of professionalism and integrity. SOPs and checklists represent your 'Box of Standards' and are there for your safety and the safety of others. Use them without deviation.

People, equipment and facilities

Additionally, the single-pilot will more often than not participate with a client who may be on board, on the ground or in support. This all requires good CRM to manage the available resources, including people, equipment and facilities.

> **Example**

Consider a pilot working for the Rural Fire Service conducting water bombing operations. Even though the pilot is the only person on board the aircraft, his "crew" actually includes:

- the refueler
- the dispatcher operating the radios for SAR
- the Fire Boss
- the fire crews on the ground
- the ground support staff helping the pilot
- other pilots working in the same area, etc.

The pilot then has to manage all of this crew to facilitate a successful flight. This can take a lot of skill and experience to manage. Most of this has to be managed individually by the pilot, however, with some delegation, the pilot can share his workload.

The refueler should have some knowledge of the fuel capacity of the aircraft and be familiar with how the fuel cap is placed on and off and the standard signals used to start and stop fuel delivery.

The dispatcher can prompt the pilot for SAR times and keep track of where he is.

The Fire Boss can tell the pilot where to go and tell him where the other helicopters are for separation.

The fire crews on the ground can help guide the pilot to the correct spot.

The ground staff can ensure the pilot receives sufficient water and food and has a break. They look after some of the little things like cleaning the aircraft window or securing a seat, or loading and unloading the helicopter. The ground staff will also managethe rigging of sling loads, calculate the weight and work with the pilot even though he is on the ground.

Other pilots operating in the same environment can talk to each other to maintain alert levels, speak up if they notice something unusual and inform each other of obstacles and hazards.

This is all part of CRM for the single pilot, allowing all the principles stated above, even though they may relate more to a multi-crew environment, to be applied equally for the single pilot.

What could possibly happen?

https://www.youtube.com/watch?v=e2qmowj9duU

Decision-Making Techniques

What is decision making?

"Decision-making is rendering a solution to a problem and defining a plan of action.

Decision-making must involve risk assessment and management".

Quality of decision making

The quality of decision making and problem-solving throughout the planning and execution phases of the sortie depend on:

- the information available
- the time constraints
- the level of involvement and information exchange among crew members.

Key decision maker

The crew's ability to apply appropriate decision-making techniques based on these criteria has a major impact on the choice and quality of their resultant actions. It is important to note that although the entire crew should be involved in the decision making and problem-solving process, the aircraft captain is the key decision-maker.

Risk elements

During each flight, decisions must be made regarding events involving interactions between the four risk elements:

- the pilot in command
- the aircraft
- the environment
- the operation.

The decision-making process involves an evaluation of each of these risk elements to achieve an accurate perception of the flight situation.

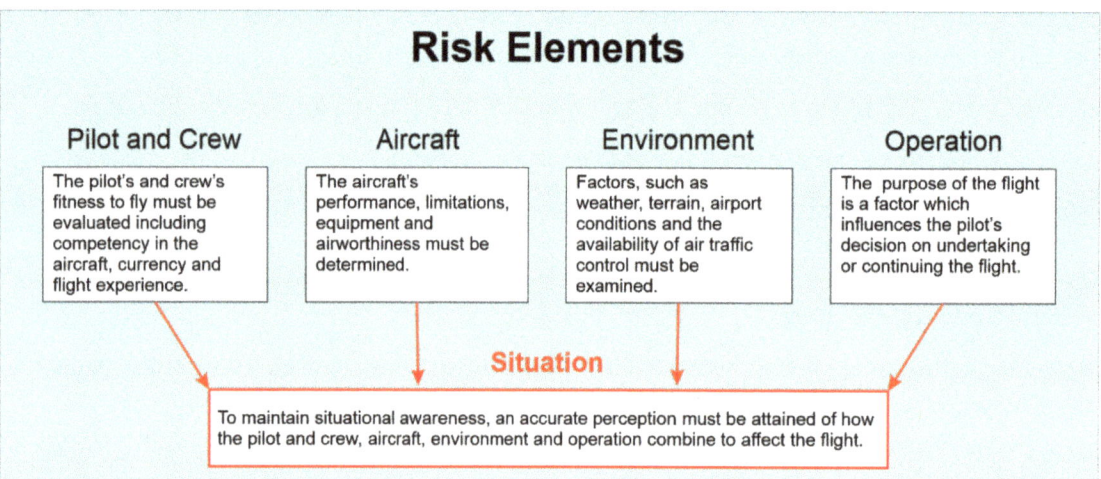

Process

Steps for good decision-making are:

1. Identifying personal attitudes hazardous to safe flight.
2. Learning behaviour modification techniques.
3. Learning how to recognise and cope with stress.
4. Developing risk assessment skills.
5. Using all resources.
6. Evaluating the effectiveness of one's decision-making skills.

 **Article: Appendix 2: Improved Aeronautical Decision Making Can Reduce Accidents**

3Ps Model

Making a risk assessment is important, but in order to make any assessment, the pilot must be able to see and sense surroundings and process what is seen before performing corrective action. An excellent process to use in this scenario is called the 3Ps: Perceive, Process, and Perform.

The 3Ps model refers to **Perceive-Process-Perform**, which is a simple and systematic approach that can be used for all phases of flight (FAA, 2016)[13].

Pilots have to:

- "perceive" the given set of circumstances for a flight
- "process" by evaluating their impact on flight safety
- "perform" by implementing the best course of action.

This 3P process begins anew with every set of circumstances as they occur during the flight. This model is a continuous loop to keep pilots vigilant and proactive in maintaining safe flight.

DECIDE Model

The DECIDE Model for Aeronautical Decision Making (ADM) is a six-step process that provides a logical way to approach decision making (FAA, 2016).

This deductive reasoning model is taught to accomplish good ADM and is useful for novice pilots but doesn't necessarily represent advanced decision-making abilities used by expert pilots. This is because of the significant difference that exists between the mental processing carried out by novices compared to experts in how they approach problem-solving and decision making.

Despite this, the DECIDE model does enhance the conventional decision making for novice pilots by increasing pilot awareness, teaching the ability to search for and establish relevant information, as well as raising motivational levels used to choose, execute and monitor actions, thus leading to a safer process.

The six steps are as follows:

- **Detect:** Detection of changes
- **Estimate:** Estimate the need for countermeasures or reactions to the change
- **Choose:** Choose a safe outcome
- **Identify:** Identification of actions that will successfully control the change
- **Do:** Implement the chosen actions
- **Evaluate:** Evaluate the effect of action in countering the change and progress of the flight.

GRADE Model

The **GRADE** loop is a simpler reasoning model that may help to determine a course of action in complex circumstances.

- **Gather:** Ensure that you have all the information that you need about the situation.
- **Review:** State the situation and ensure that everybody agrees.
- **Analyse:** Determine a suitable solution based on the information available.
- **Decide:** State a decision and a plan of action. Remember that ultimately, the decision lies with the PIC, particularly if there are conflicting opinions.
- **Evaluate:** Don't be afraid to review the decision if circumstances change or you learn more about a situation.

---

[13] FAA (2016), Pilot's Handbook of Aeronautical Knowledge, Chapter 2 Aeronautical Decision Making, https://www.faa.gov/sites/faa.gov/files/2022-03/pilot_handbook.pdf

Analytical decision making

When under pressure, especially time pressure, pilots may make decisions in automatic mode, short-cutting key steps, assessing only one or two outcomes and sticking to what feels familiar and taking the first workable solution they find.

The DECIDE model encourages an analytical decision-making process, as illustrated in the diagram below.

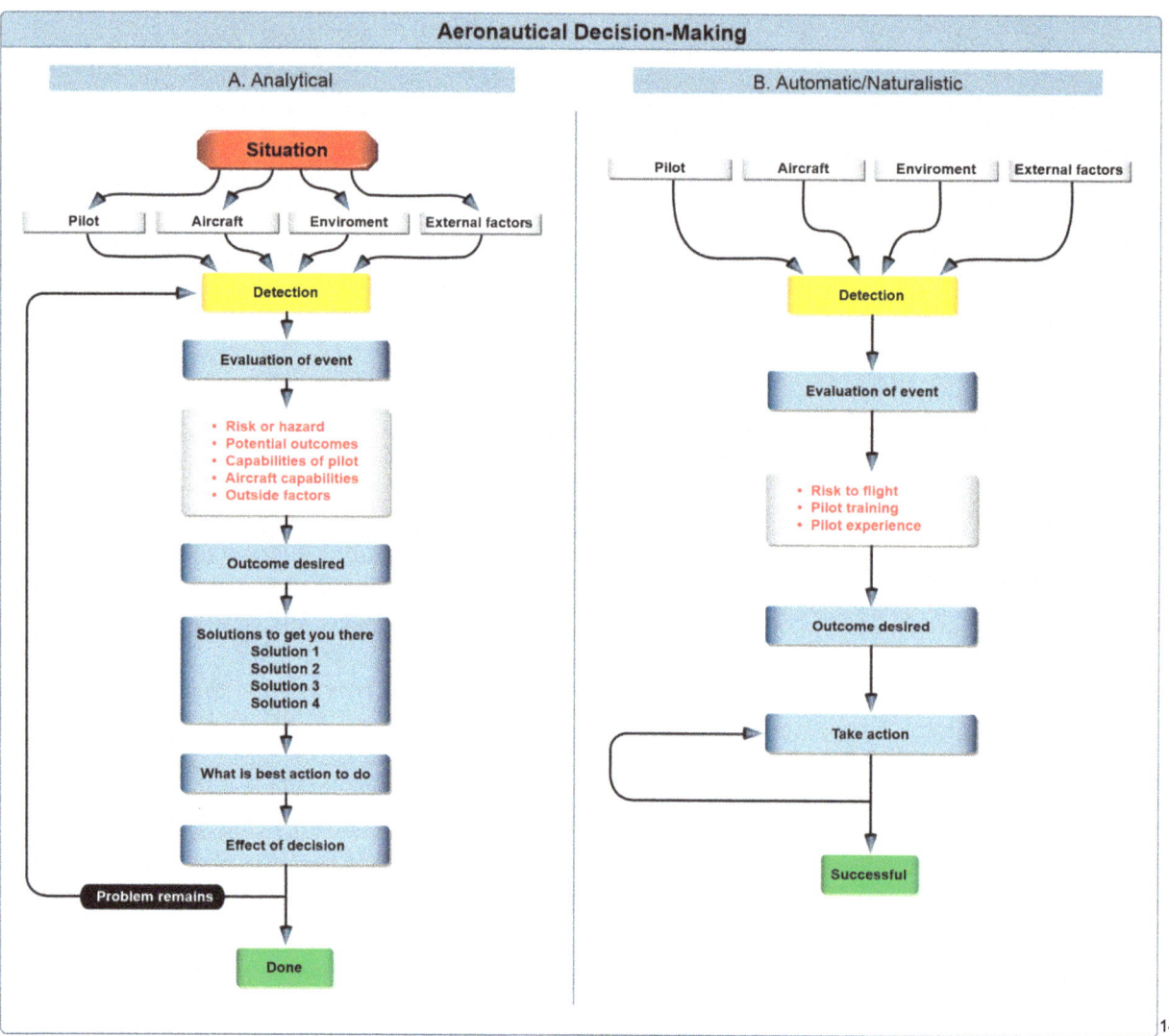

Get-There-itis

In 'get-there-it is', personal or external pressure clouds the vision and impairs judgment by causing a fixation on the original goal or destination combined with a total disregard for alternative courses of action.

For example, "I have to be back at base by 1500".

If you feel time pressure, take a moment to decide if it's real or self-induced. You may be in a hurry to save a life, in which case taking a risk may be justified.

If you're suffering from self-induced pressure, or feel pressure from the organisation to achieve a task within a set timeframe, then don't cut corners. Better to arrive late than never.

> Tip: Intuition is a powerful tool for an experienced pilot.
> If something feels wrong, your brain is trying to tell you something.
> Take the extra time to double-check.

---

[14] FAA (2016), Pilot's Handbook of Aeronautical Knowledge, Aeronautical Decision-Making, p. 2-19, https://www.faa.gov/sites/faa.gov/files/2022-03/pilot_handbook.pdf

Attitude

How a pilot handles his or her responsibilities as a pilot depends on attitude. Attitudes can be developed through training into a mental framework that encourages good pilot judgment.

Hazardous attitudes can lead to poor decision making and actions that involve unnecessary risk. The pilot must examine decisions carefully to ensure that the choices have not been influenced by hazardous attitudes and be familiar with positive alternatives to counteract the hazardous attitudes.

These substitute attitudes are referred to as antidotes. During a flight operation, it is important to recognize a hazardous attitude, correctly label the thought, and then recall its antidote.

During multi-pilot operations, the presence of other crew members may not protect you. Remember, as a PIC, you still lead by example, and the reaction of your crew will depend on their personalities, experience levels and your relationship with them.

Hazardous Attitudes

- **Macho**
  Some people need to always prove that they are better than anyone else and take risks to prove themselves and impress others.
- **Anti-authority**
  Some people do not like anyone telling them what to do.
- **Invulnerability**
  Some people feel that accidents happen to other people but never to themselves. Pilots who think like this are more likely to take unwise risks.
- **Impulsivity**
  Some people need to do something, anything, immediately without stopping to think about what is the best action to take.
- **Resignation**
  Some people do not see themselves as making a great deal of difference in what happens to them and will go along with anything that happens.

Hazardous Attitudes	Antidotes
Macho – Steve often brags to his friends about his skills as a pilot and how close to the ground he flies. During a local pleasure flight in his single-engine airplane, he decides to buzz some friends barbecuing at a nearby park.	**Taking chances is foolish.**
Anti-Authority – Although he knows that flying so low to the ground is prohibited by the regulations, he feels that the regulations are too restrictive in some circumstances.	**Follow the rules. They are usually right.**
Invulnerability – Steve is not worried about an accident since he has flown this low many times before, and he has not had any problems.	**It could happen to me.**
Impulsivity – As he is buzzing the park, the airplane does not climb as well as Steve had anticipated, and without thinking, Steve pulls back hard on the yoke. The airspeed drops, and the airplane is close to a stalling attitude as the wing brushes a power line.	**Not so fast. Think first.**
Resignation – Although Steve manages to recover, the wing sustains minor damage. Steve thinks to himself, "It's dangerous for the power company to put those lines so close to a park. If somebody finds out about this I'm going to be in trouble, but it seems like no matter what I do, somebody's always going to criticise."	**I'm not helpless. I can make a difference.**

Operational Pitfalls

There are a number of classic behavioural traps into which pilots have been known to fall. Pilots, particularly those with considerable experience, as a rule, always try to complete a flight as planned, please passengers, and meet schedules. The basic drive to meet or exceed goals can have an adverse effect on safety, and can impose an unrealistic assessment of piloting skills under stressful conditions.

These tendencies ultimately may bring about practices that are dangerous and often illegal and may lead to a mishap. A pilot will develop awareness and learn to avoid many of these operational pitfalls through effective ADM training.

Peer Pressure	Poor decision making may be based upon an emotional response to peers, rather than evaluating a situation objectively.
Mind Set	A pilot displays a mindset through an inability to recognise and cope with changes in a given situation.
Get-There-Itis	This disposition impairs pilot judgement through a fixation on the original goal or destination, combined with a disregard for any alternative course of action.
Duck-Under Syndrome	A pilot may be tempted to make it into an airport by descending below minimums during an approach. There may be a belief that there is a built-in margin of error in every approach procedure, or a pilot may not want to admit that the landing cannot be completed and a missed approach must be initiated.
Scud Running	Scud running occurs when a pilot tries to maintain visual contact with the terrain at low altitudes while instrument conditions exist.
Continuing Visual Flight Rules (VFR) into Instrument Conditions	Spatial disorientation or collision with ground/obstacles may occur when a pilot continues VFR into instrument conditions. This can be even more dangerous if the pilot is not instrument-rated or current.
Getting Behind the Aircraft	This pitfall can be caused by allowing events or situations to control pilot actions. A constant state of surprise at what happens next may be exhibited when the pilot gets behind the aircraft.
Loss of Positional or Situational Awareness	In extreme cases, when a pilot gets behind the aircraft, a loss of positional or situational awareness may result. The pilot may not know the aircraft's geographical location or may be unable to recognise deteriorating circumstances.
Operating Without Adequate Fuel Reserves	Ignoring minimum fuel reserve requirements is generally the result of overconfidence, lack of flight planning, or disregarding applicable regulations.
Descent Below the Minimum En-Route Altitude	The duck-under syndrome, as mentioned above, can also occur during the en-route portion of an IFR flight.
Flying Outside the Envelope	The assumed high-performance capability of a particular aircraft may cause a mistaken belief that it can meet the demands imposed by a pilot's overestimated flying skills.
Neglect of Flight planning, Pre-flight Inspections and Checklists	A pilot may rely on short and long term memory, regular flying skills, and familiar routes instead of established procedures and published checklists. This can be particularly true of experienced pilots.

Phraseology

Below is a list of standard phraseology used in the multi-crew environment.

Phrase	Definition
Abort	Terminate a pre-planned manoeuvre or sortie.
All clear	An announcement that the area called by the applicable crew member is clear of obstacles or traffic. It may be followed by the position in the aircraft for multi-crew. For example, "all clear back left".
Back left/right	Refers to the position in the aircraft the crewmember is calling from in the back of the aircraft.
Braking	An announcement by FP or PM who intends to apply brake pressure (wheeled aircraft only)
Break left/right/up/down	An immediate action command to perform an emergency manoeuvre to deviate from the present track
Call out	Command from either AC or FP for a specified procedure to be read from the checklist by another member of the crew
Caution	Used in conjunction with a Warning. It allows other crewmembers to develop a mental picture of what is happening during an approach/departure when manoeuvring around a pad or persons/vehicles within the vicinity of the landing area. For example: "Caution wires" or "Caution dust."
Check Altitude	An announcement by any crewmember for the FP to immediately check the altitude/height AMSL or AGL as appropriate for the mission profile
Check Balance	An announcement by any crewmember for the FP to immediately check balance
Check Heading	An announcement by any crewmember for the FP to immediately check the heading
Check Nav	An announcement by any crewmember or another aircraft crew for the FP and PM to immediately check their current position and heading to target (check your navigation)
Check Power	An announcement by any crewmember for the FP to immediately check the power/torque setting
Check RPM	An announcement by any crewmember for the FP to immediately check the RPM (primarily rotor RPM but also engine RPM, both N1 and N2)
Check Speed	An announcement by any crewmember for the FP to immediately check the airspeed (or ground speed determined by the mission profile)
Come up/down	Command to change the altitude up or down
Controls	Aircraft flight controls

Phrase	Definition
Distance to run	Distance information referring to the distance in nautical miles, feet or metres from the aircraft to the desired target, set down point or obstacles on the approach path
Drifting left/right, forward/aft/backwards	An alert of the unintentional or undirected movement of the aircraft while at the hover, it will be followed by the direction of the movement. For example, drifting left refers to the helicopter drifting to the left. The FP should immediately stop the movement.
Egress	Emergency command to evacuate the aircraft
Execute	Initiate an action previously discussed
Expect	Anticipate further instructions or guidance
Expedite	A command to take action immediately. This is normally directed by Air Traffic Control or an aircrew member putting urgency into their request For example: Expedite crossing the runway. Means to do it immediately without hesitation.
Eyes inside	The primary focus of the announcing crewmember is inside the aircraft for an extended period of time, and obstacle clearance duties for that crew position need to be reallocated to another crewmember.
Eyes outside	The primary focus of the announcing crewmember is back outside the aircraft, and obstacle clearance duties for that crew position are accepted.
Fly heading	Command to fly an assigned compass heading
Front left/right	Referring to the position in the aircraft the crewmember is calling from in the front of the aircraft.
Go	The command to initiate an action previously discussed. This is a shortened version of the command "execute." For example: Quick stop - GO
Handing over	An announcement by the FP that he is handing over the controls to the PM and that they will now swap roles
Height below the aircraft/load	An estimation of the height below the aircraft or external load to the closest obstacles on the approach angle or to the ground. Usually given in feet or metres.
Hold	A command given by a crew member to ensure any aircraft movement is stopped immediately.
I have control	A statement by the FP that he now has control of the aircraft.
Jettison	Command for the emergency release of an external load or stores.
Landing on	Prior to descending from a stabilised hover to land on the surface, the FP should call "Landing on."

Phrase	Definition
Lifting	Prior to raising collective and lifting to a hover the FP should call "*Lifting*"
Lines good	An announcement by a crew member to the FP that the current line the helicopter is following is clear of obstacles to the termination point
Looking	An announcement that the crewmember is looking for the target, traffic, or obstacle as requested by air traffic of another crewmember and that it is not yet positively sighted or identified
Losing sight	The point at which the FP has lost sight of the termination point and requires the aircrewman to commence providing advice for the position the aircraft clear of obstacles
Maintain	Command to continue or keep the same
Maintain your height	A command given by the appropriate crewmember (the one who can see the terrain or obstacle the best) when it appears that the aircraft if it continues on the same line, will encroach safety limits to obstacles if the current height is not maintained
Monitor	Command to maintain constant watch or observation. This could be to monitor a particular instrument or radio or obstacle etc.
Move	Command to hover "forward, aft, left or right" followed by a distance For example, move forward 20 metres
Move left/right on line	A command given during an approach to a pad if the aircraft is left or right of the line required to remain clear of obstacles on the approach path. Once the desired line is acquired, the call "Line's good" is given
Negative	Incorrect or permission not granted or no
Nil / negative contact	Unable to establish communications
Not sighted	Target, traffic, or obstacle not positively seenor identified
Now	Immediate action is required
Passengers (crew) clear in/out	Command to have personnel enter or exit the aircraft or rotor disc area
Release	A command for the planned or expected release of an external load or store
Roger	Message received and understood
Say again	Repeat your transmission
Set in back	Call given when the aircrewman has completed cabin safety checks of passengers, cargo security, loose articles, door security and personal harnesses
Sighted	Target, traffic, or obstacle is positively seen or identified

Phrase	Definition
Sliding left/right	An announcement by the FP of the intentional sideways movement left or right at the hover
Slow down	Command to decrease airspeed (sometimes groundspeed depending on the mission profile)
Speed up	Command to increase airspeed (sometimes groundspeed depending on the mission profile)
Standby	Wait – duties of higher priority are being performed, and the request cannot be complied with at this time
Stop	Command to go no further – cease the present action
Taking over	Command by the AC assuming control of his/her aircraft. The term is also used as an acknowledgment of duties being assumed for a particular crewmember's activity after he/she has used the term Handing Over
Traffic	Refers to friendly aircraft that presents a potential hazard to the current route of flight; will be followed by an approximate clock position and the distance from the aircraft with reference to altitude
Turn	Command to deviate from the present ground track; will be followed by words left or right and clock ray indication for low-level flight (to ensure FP does not bring attention inside the aircraft) or compass heading
Turning Left/Right	Prior to the FP commencing a turn the FP should announce "Turning Left/Right"
Unable	Indicates the inability to comply with a specific instruction or request
Up on	Indicates primary radio selected; will be followed by radio selector position
Wilco	Message received and understood, and I will comply
You have control	An announcement by the FP that he is no longer the FP and that the FP and PM have swapped roles

Multi-Crew Cooperation *for Helicopter Pilots*

Case Study

A Case Study

The following case study follows a multi-engine, multi-crew IFR S76 reposition flight in the USA[15].

Article: Appendix 3: Air Ambulance Strikes Terrain After Takeoff in Fog

Ask yourself

When reading, take note of the events and write down;

1. The mistakes you think the crew made, and
2. What would you do differently?
3. Could they have saved themselves?

Summary

Video: John Nance

https://www.youtube.com/watch?v=5qDalK9-HH8

All crew members' input is essential.

Communicate effectively.

Take the time.

---

[15] FSF Editorial Staff (March-April 2003), Air Ambulance Strikes Terrain After Takeoff in Flog, Flight Safety Foundation, Helicopter Safety, Vol. 29 No. 2, https://flightsafety.org/hs/hs_mar-apr03.pdf

Multi-Crew Cooperation (MCC)

MCC Definition

"MCC is the ability of the Flight Crew to operate as a team using Standard Operating Procedures (SOPs) in a particular aircraft type to ensure its safe operation."

Flight Crew Definition

The Flight Crew represents the two (2) pilots in the cockpit who are occupying the control seats and who together are either manipulating the flight controls or managing the aircraft's systems in the conduct of the flight.

CASA definition

The term 'Multi-Crew Cooperation' is defined in the Australian Civil Aviation Safety Regulations as an operation that requires at least two pilots in:

- a multi-crew aircraft (that is, the aircraft is certificated for operation by a crew of at least two pilots by the manufacturer); or
- an aircraft that is equipped, and required by the regulations, to be operated by a crew of at least two pilots.

Operations Manual

Unfortunately, by definition, an aircraft that is operated by two pilots, but does not comply with one of the definitions above, is not at present deemed a multi-crew operation by CASA. This includes IFR and NVG.

This interpretation may be over-ruled by a Company's Operations Manual if it contains Standard Operating Procedures (SOPs) to operate an aircraft as a multi-crew operation regardless of its certification.

This interpretation may also change over time as CASA understands and fully recognises how helicopter operators are working as multi-crew.

MCC Core Principles

Basic training

A new pilot will typically learn to fly a simple helicopter. These simple helicopters usually have one engine, minimal systems to manage and can easily be flown by a single pilot. The flying and the operation are usually simple and designed to give the new pilot the hands and feet skills (often referred to as stick and rudder) to fly and the general knowledge to manage a flight.

Commercial needs

Having acquired the basic flying skills and obtaining a licence, it quickly becomes obvious that most commercial operators and employers have more advanced needs and typically use bigger, more sophisticated helicopters to conduct more complex operations.

Higher qualifications

A pilot may now need to be able to operate at night or in IMC and so must gain an instrument rating; there may become a requirement to fly using a Night Vision Imaging System (NVIS) with a limited field of view. Helicopters often have complex role equipment such as a hoist or FLIR or a customer may require a two-pilot crew to transfer its employees safely offshore.

Operate the aircraft

As pilots are expected to operate more complex aircraft or simple aircraft in a more complex way, piloting becomes more challenging and more demanding.

No longer can a pilot simply concentrate on flying the helicopter; instead, the crew together must "*operate*" the aircraft.

---

[16] Camphin, Michael D. https://www.pexels.com/photo/yellow-helicopter-2906726/ (Creative Commons)

[17] By SSgt Elizabeth Rissmiller [Public domain], via Wikimedia Commons https://upload.wikimedia.org/wikipedia/commons/a/a3/U.S._Army_MH-47G_Chinook_helicopter_pilots_perform_preflight_operations_during_Emerald_Warrior_2013_at_Hurlburt_Field%2C_Fla.%2C_April_29%2C_2013_130429-F-MN146-197.jpg

Benefits of MCC

The more complex the helicopter or, the more complex the operation, the more support a pilot needs. Having two (2) pilots in the cockpit will mean each can help the other to:

- Cope with challenging operating conditions
- Navigate and operate the radios
- Manage aircraft systems
- Operate roll equipment (hoist, FLIR, night sun, etc.)
- Assist in an emergency
- Provide rest and help in managing fatigue
- Deal with payloads and passengers
- Fly to the required tolerances
- Deal with differences in experience levels
- Have a second opinion and additional input when major decisions need to be made

Another benefit of MCC is the ability for junior pilots to be mentored and trained by a senior pilot so that, in time, they will themselves become senior pilots.

MCC origins

MCC training had its origins as a requirement for ATPL fixed-wing pilots. These pilots would predominantly fly fixed routes carrying fare-paying passengers in larger airliners. With several hundred people on board a single airplane, sound multi-crew skills are important to help improve safety and reduce the risk of an accident or incident bought about by human error.

Working as a team

By controlling flight deck interactions, teaching CRM and developing standard operating procedures (SOPs), the crew can function as a coherent team.

Helicopter MCC

MCC is also applicable to many helicopter operations; however, when compared to fixed-wing operations, helicopter MCC can have some significant differences.

The majority of commercial MCC fixed-wing operations repeat the same route and type of flying with very little variation from day to day. This means MCC procedures can be very static and predictable.

Helicopter operations have a far greater possibility for variation. Not only can the routes vary from flight to flight, but also the types of operation that the crews may be tasked to conduct can have some dramatic variations. As helicopters operate in a very different environment from fixed-wing aircraft, the MCC emphasis is also different. Fixed-wing safety is improved by tackling automation use through the application of SOP. Helicopter safety is improved by tackling situational awareness and CRM through the application of SOP.

---

18 Fae (2018), QANTAS 767 to Melbourne, https://commons.wikimedia.org/wiki/File:QANTAS_to_Melbourne-01%2B_(267472290).jpg (Creative Commons 2.0)

Multi-Crew Cooperation *for Helicopter Pilots*

Example

Consider the differences between an airliner flying on a set route from one city to another compared to a helicopter that may be tasked to do a search and rescue over an unknown route, departing from a road and landing on a hospital helipad while transiting using NVGs and operating under the IFR.

Emergencies

In addition, an emergency in a helicopter can be very different compared to a fixed-wing aircraft. For the most threatening emergencies (fires, engine failures and undesired aircraft states), pilot reaction speeds may need to be much faster, and some reactions (for example, entering autorotation or recovering from VRS) needs to be instinctive and automatic which do not lend themselves to a lengthy discussion between the crew or the active use of an emergency checklist.

For some emergencies, the helicopter pilot has an option that the fixed-wing pilot does not have, that is the ability to land almost anywhere. Unfortunately, on the other hand, many technical failures on a helicopter have catastrophic consequences or do not lend themselves to scenarios where crews have time to plan and discuss options while proceeding to an airfield.

This means that the requirement to manage an emergency, manage systems, optimise performance and constantly re-plan to take an aircraft to a successful landing area can be very different for a helicopter pilot, who ultimately may have the low-risk option of simply landing immediately into an unprepared landing site that must be achieved so quickly that the helicopter pilot will not be able to apply high-quality multi-crew co-operation.

---

[19] https://commons.wikimedia.org/wiki/File:CCLoadingPt.jpg (Public Domain)

[20] http://www.africareview.com/image/view/-/1429972/highRes/371386/-/maxh/283/maxw/432/-/pxlyv3/-/chopperpix.jpg

[21] https://commons.wikimedia.org/wiki/File:Talamanca_de_Jarama_1985.jpg

Situational Awareness

On the other hand, helicopters frequently operate at low levels, in to confined landing areas and at night. Reviewing fatal helicopter accidents on multi-pilot helicopters caused by human factors shows a clear trend of accidents caused by a lack of situational awareness, spatial disorientation or poor CRM applied in demanding circumstances. It is these skills that the helicopter pilot who has cut his teeth flying single-pilot operations must learn to work within a multi-crew environment.

Summary

In summary, this means successful multi-crew operations in a helicopter can look quite different from those in a fixed-wing aircraft.

The MCC reference material provided here is structured to talk about many aspects of crew cooperation in general. However, because of the variety of roles that a helicopter can perform, it would be impossible to cover every scenario and eventuality. These notes, therefore, exist to give a firm grounding in theory and practice to increase awareness and teach lessons for future application in real-world operations.

Shared Responsibilities

A key aspect of multi-crew operations is the sharing of responsibilities. This includes each pilot having the ability to divide their time between **_flying_** the aircraft or **_monitoring_** systems and communications. During single-pilot operations, the pilot is responsible for all aspects of the aircraft's operation. During multi-crew operations, the crew roles are separated and shared. One pilot will always be **_flying_** the aircraft while the other will **monitor** the flight and assist. _Both_ are responsible for monitoring and cross-checking each other, so good communication is key to doing this effectively.

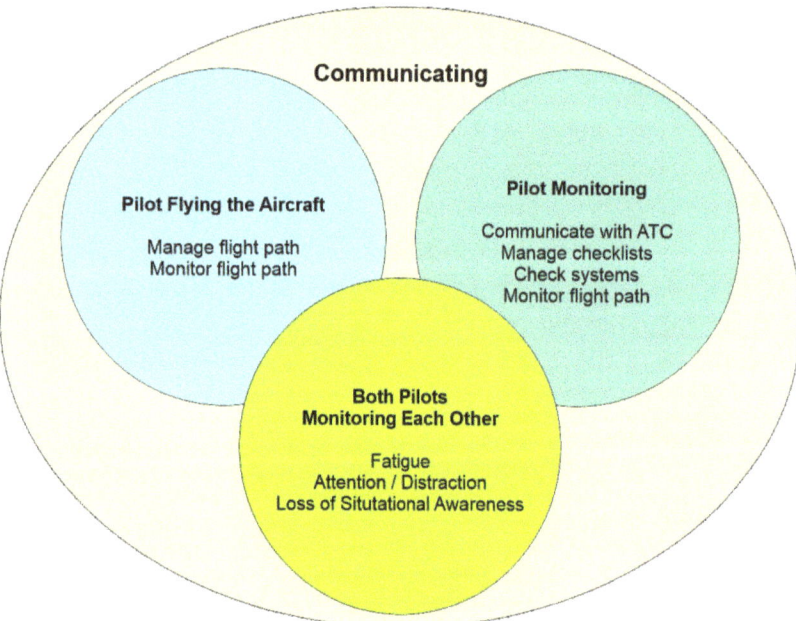

Shared responsibilities

The time flying the aircraft and monitoring the flight is shared for many reasons, including:

- The division and sharing of the workload
- The ability to focus or concentration on a specific task
- Making best use of the experience of each individual pilot
- The ability to mentor, impart knowledge and skills, providing training or gaining experience
- Providing capacity for shared decision making with the ability to have more input and conversation about decisions
- Managing and ultimately reducing the mental and physical fatigue of each pilot

This MCC guide will help to identify tools and techniques to achieve these results.

Multi-Crew Cooperation *for Helicopter Pilots*

Crew Positions

For any flight, the crew will be designated specific crew positions. This is important to know prior to the flight so that a proper cockpit gradient can exist and the crew can function with known roles and responsibilities.

Types of positions

There are two (2) types of positions that can be allocated, they are:

1. The *Executive Positions* such as the Captain and the Co-Pilot.
   These Executive Positions are assigned prior to the flight and continue throughout the flight without change until the de-brief is completed, and
2. The *Operating Positions* which allows each pilot to be either the **P**ilot **F**lying (**PF**) or **P**ilot **M**onitoring (**PM**).
   These Operating Positions can change throughout the flight at the discretion of the Captain or in accordance with the Company's SOPs.

Each of these positions is classified as a *Role* with each role having specific *Responsibilities*.

Role

A role is a fixed position that cannot be shared or delegated.

The Roles available in the cockpit are;

- The Captain and the Co-Pilot, referred to as the Executive Positions
- The Pilot Flying (PF) and the Pilot Monitoring (PM), referred to as the Operating Positions

For example: There can only be one Captain at a time, and there can only be one Pilot Flying (PF) at a time. The Roles cannot be shared at any one time.

Responsibility

A Responsibility, or more correctly, multiple Responsibilities, come with each Role.

In general, responsibilities will be attached to a Role to avoid confusion and set standards. However, some responsibilities may be shared or delegated during a flight depending on the circumstances.

Executive responsibilities (Captain and Co-Pilot) cannot be delegated or shared, whereas Operating responsibilities can be delegated or shared as necessary.

For example:

The Captain is always accountable for the conduct of the flight that is a core responsibility of the role.

The Pilot Monitoring (PM) may delegate the responsibility of monitoring the radios to the Pilot Flying (PF) in some circumstances to help share the workload at a busy time.

Crew Position Matrix

These Roles and responsibilities can be described in a table as follows;

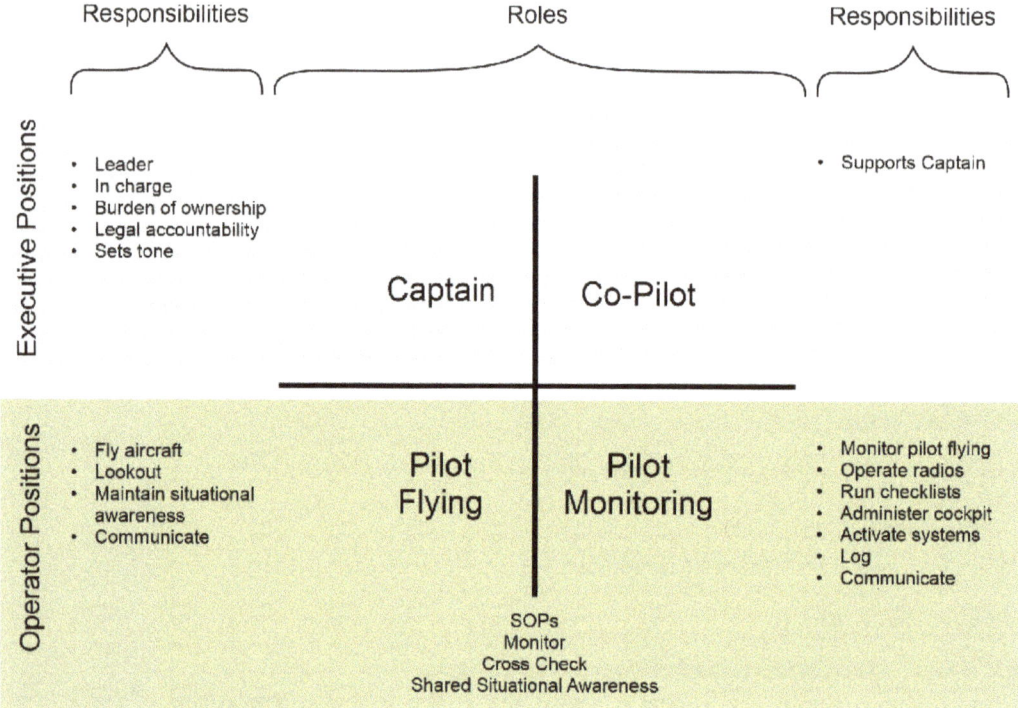

Executive Positions

The Captain

For each flight, there will be a designated Captain.

The Captain can be described by using several different words depending on the Company or Military organisation's method of identifying the role.

These different words may include but not be limited to;

- Captain
- 1st Pilot
- Pilot in Command (PIC)

Acceptance of the Role

No pilot may accept the designation as the Captain unless having the required qualifications and training, the recent experience requirements and the knowledge required to conduct the flight and is considered in all respects competent and fit for the task.

Responsibilities of the role

The Captain:

- must be one of the pilots of the flight
- may nominate who is to be the PF and PM for each stage of the flight
- may be the PF or the PM
- may delegate the conduct of the flight to the Co-Pilot but remains the overall PIC of the flight
- will delegate specific tasks that either the Captain or Co-Pilot will need to complete on the ground in order to successfully prepare for and manage the flight
- may, in exceptional circumstances, (for example, becomes sick) designate another pilot or the Co-Pilot as the PIC for the remainder of the flight
- is the pilot in charge and responsible for the overall operation and safety of the aircraft and its payload
- is responsible for ensuring cockpit roles are effectively delegated and the use of crew resources is optimal.

When considering the "cockpit gradient" (who is in charge and has the authority to make decisions in an aircraft), the Captain ultimately carries the responsibility of command and for decisions made during flight and ground operations.

The Co-Pilot

For each flight, there will be a designated Co-Pilot.

The Co-Pilot can be described by using several different words depending on the Company or Units method of identifying the role.

These different words may include but not be limited to;

- Co-Pilot
- 2nd Pilot
- Second in Command (SIC) or
- First Officer

Acceptance of the Role

No pilot may accept the designation as the Co-Pilot unless having the required qualifications and training, the recent experience requirements and the knowledge required to conduct the flight and is considered in all respects competent and fit for the task.

Responsibilities of the role

The Co-Pilot:

- must be one of the pilots of the flight
- may be the PF or the PM
- will complete any delegated tasks given by the Captain in order to successfully prepare for and manage the flight
- may act as the PIC if designated to do so under the supervision of the Captain; this is referred to as In Command Under Supervision (ICUS) and allows the Co-Pilot to practice being in command.
- in exceptional circumstances (for example, the PIC becomes sick), can be designated PIC for the remainder of the flight.
- is the pilot supporting the Captain and will help in managing the overall operation and safety of the aircraft and its payload.

When considering the "cockpit gradient" (who is in charge and has the authority to make decisions in an aircraft), the Co-Pilot is empowered to provide guidance, support and input to make decisions for which the Captain is ultimately responsible.

Assigning Executive Positions

Company or Military Unit

Executive positions can be assigned in a number of different ways, but primarily the decision is either made by the Company or Military Unit through employment agreements, SOPs and legal requirements.

Failing this method, the decision can be made between the pilots themselves before the commencement of the flight.

Most common method

The most common method is to have the most experienced or qualified pilot as the Pilot In Command.

In this scenario, the authority gradient as it exists will be clear, and it will primarily be the job of the Captain to exercise good leadership and the Co-Pilot to exercise good followership.

Other possibilities

There are a number of other possibilities that also need to be considered where the designation of the Captain may not be clear; these include:

- Two pilots with similar experience levels
- A less experienced pilot with more experience on the aircraft type compared to an experienced pilot with only limited time on the aircraft type
- One experienced pilot and one less experienced pilot who are both qualified as Captains but are doing 'time about' between each leg

These scenarios can bring the most challenges as the cockpit authority gradient can be unclear, or the possibility exists that the gradient can change during a task.

The strategies used to resolve this potential conflict comes down to culture, personality experience, SOPs and ultimately, the ability to communicate well.

Rules

There are two rules that, when applied, help to ensure that the task begins on the right foot:

1. Explicitly acknowledge during the planning and pre-flight briefing which is the Pilot in Command. Do not step towards the aircraft unless both pilots are absolutely clear on this point.
2. Understand that the designation of a Captain is crucial to a functioning cockpit authority gradient.

Crew Flight Positions

Two new positions

Multi-crew Cooperation operations bring two new crew roles into the cockpit.

They are the

- Pilot Flying (PF)
- Pilot Monitoring (PM).

These positions allow each pilot to swap between the PF and PM Roles as required, sometimes frequently, during a flight.

MCC training includes understanding how the PF and PM share tasks and support each other in successful helicopter operations.

Pilot Flying (PF)

The Pilot Flying (PF) is responsible for operating the flight controls directly or through the autopilot to control the aircraft to manage the aircraft's height, heading and speed.

The PF can be either the Captain or Co-Pilot, depending who has been delegated this responsibility at the time.

The Pilot Flying can go by several different names, including;

- Pilot Flying (PF)
- Flying Pilot (FP).

---

[22] http://www.af.mil/News/Photos.aspx?igphoto=2000366631 (public domain)

[23] https://commons.wikimedia.org/wiki/File:Bell212Pilot0001.png (public domain)

Pilot Monitoring (PM)

The Pilot Monitoring (PM) is responsible for providing support and direction to the Pilot Flying (PF). The PM is not operating the flight controls directly or through the autopilot, instead the PM will be required to:

- monitor the PF and give advice and direction when necessary
- monitor the aircrafts flight path
- manage the radios and navigation equipment
- manage checklists
- manage aircraft systems.

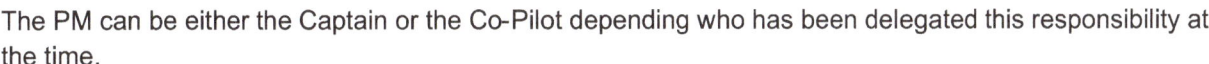

The PM is there to support the PF.

The PM can be either the Captain or the Co-Pilot depending who has been delegated this responsibility at the time.

The Pilot Monitoring can go by several different names, including:

- Pilot Monitoring (PM)
- Non-Flying Pilot (NFP)
- Pilot Assisting (PA).

Awareness of Abilities

To effectively manage a cockpit, both pilots must be aware of each other's abilities. Some of this is assumed knowledge based on gaining qualifications and the completion of Company or Military Unit check rides and signoffs.

This is why crews can be rostered, having never actually flown together in the past. However, the best functioning crews are the ones that have worked together for some time as their full abilities, strengths and weaknesses are then known to each other.

Traditional model

Traditionally, it fell to the Captain to know and be aware of the limitations of the Co-Pilot delegating cockpit roles, with the unspoken assumption that the Captain could take care of their self without any help from the Co-Pilot.

The Captain's cone of knowledge, experience and skill is typically larger than the Co-Pilot's cone of knowledge, experience and skill.

Figure 6 Traditional Pilot / Co-Pilot Model

At the same time, the existence of this assumed cone-of-knowledge and the existence of the authority gradient means that the SIC may not be aware of the PIC's limitations, either in general or at the specific moment when the capacity of the PIC has been exhausted.

---

[24] https://commons.wikimedia.org/wiki/File:US_Navy_020709-N-4374S-011_Pilot_checks_a_navigational_chart_while_flying_an_MH-53E.jpg (public domain)

Awareness

The Captain must have an awareness of the experience, qualifications and ability of a Co-Pilot in order to achieve optimal performance and manage any particular areas of weakness, particularly if there is a clear gap in experience.

In MCC operations, the Co-Pilot should also be aware of any limitations affecting the Captain.

Similar to the Pilot In Commands authority, this awareness of ability can be explicit (written down) or implicit (assumed).

Example

Consider a Co-Pilot who has only just received a type qualification on the aircraft. The Co-Pilot may not have a good working knowledge from memory of the aircraft's systems and limitations, so the Captain will take this into consideration. This may be an example of an implicit (assumed) limitation on the Co-Pilot's abilities.

Consider a Captain who has a medical limitation, and he must fly with a Co-Pilot who holds a PIC qualification on the aircraft. This may be an example of an explicit (written or documented) limitation on the Captain's abilities.

Preflight brief

The limitations in each pilot's abilities may not be relevant to the planned task at briefing time, and nobody will expect a full run-down of flight history and specific areas of strength and weakness on each pilot before every flight. However, a key aspect of multi-crew cooperation is a willingness of the crew to make the other aware of when their experience levels, capacity, or capability is being exceeded and ask for professional assistance to optimise the operation of an aircraft.

[25]

The responsibility to acknowledge limitations lies both with the Captain and the Co-Pilot in order that one is not flying blind without the awareness of the other.

Monitoring and Appraisal

A key role for a PM is to monitor the performance of the PF.

Likewise, a key role of the PF is to monitor the performance and be aware of the PM's needs.

This monitoring takes two key forms:

- Personal performance
- Professional performance

Personal Performance

Personal monitoring of performance means being aware of the other pilot's well-being and keeping a critical eye on their workload and performance. If they suddenly become task saturated, then step in to reduce the workload; if they appear fatigued, then come up with a strategy to allow them some rest; if they are bored and underused, then find a more useful role for them.

Professional Monitoring

Professional monitoring of performance means keeping an eye on the inputs and outputs of the aircraft.

---

[25] http://www.rotaryaction.com/pages/prisoner1.html

Both the PF and PM have responsibility for different inputs and outputs, such as:

- flight path
- ATC communications
- NAVAIDS.

We monitor to ensure the safety of personnel and the aircraft. A key role of the PM is monitoring the aircraft in flight to ensure that the PF is maintaining the correct course and flight path. Likewise, the PF must listen to ATC communication and be ready to step in to help correct any errors that occur.

A key to successful performance appraisal is the manner in which it is delivered.

For ATC clearance and off-aircraft communication, the presence of a second pilot provides an opportunity to use communication and CRM to ensure shared situational awareness. If ATC passes a clearance, run an internal loop on the cockpit to ensure shared understanding before replying or confirming the clearance:

For example:

> *ATC: 'Becker 01, Turn left heading 320'*
> *PM to PF: 'left heading 320'*
> *PF to PM: 'I'm expecting a right turn now'*
> *PM to ATC: 'Confirm left 320?'*
> *ATC: 'Apologies, right turn, heading 320'*
> *PM: 'Roger, Right heading 320'*

Active monitoring

Active monitoring is using a systematic technique to check aircraft systems and configuration. Like the consistent instrument scan during instrument flight, a pilot must develop and use a monitoring scan when in the PM role.

Unlike an instrument scan, active monitoring will change depending on circumstances. Continual active monitoring will be fatiguing; the aim is not to replicate the PF's scan. Particular operating environments will lend themselves to different monitoring styles:

- IMC / IFR
- NIGHT
- Tired
- Inexperienced
- High workload

Monitoring Styles

Try to be subtle in monitoring. Maintain an active scan but a passive posture so that your body language does not lead to a breakdown in communication. In particular, try to look at your instruments rather than those of the PF (if displays are replicated), unless you are doing a cross-check.

Be aware that leaning over can convey the impression that you are over monitoring the person rather than the situation and may well give the impression of distrust, lack of confidence in the PF or 'backseat driving', delivering a negative message.

The same can be said of a pilot leaning over and putting an arm around the seat; this could be seen as babysitting and can lead to a breakdown in the cockpit dynamics.

Monitoring	Babysitting	Over Monitoring
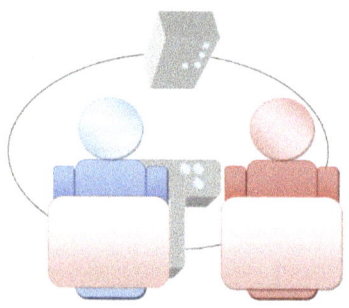	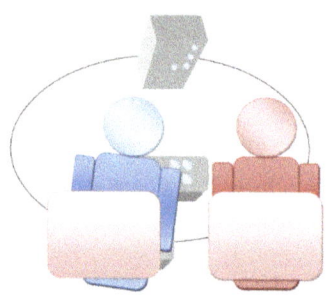	
Passive Posture Relaxed scanning Talking Mutually supporting	Leaning in Authoritative Gradient Habitual	Authority Gradient Pressure Not supporting One-way Training / Coaching

Monitoring and the Cockpit Gradient

The cockpit gradient can present challenges when monitoring. While authoritarian leaders or poor followers are the most frequent cause, sometimes more simple problems can have the worst effects.

Think about an inexperienced co-pilot flying with an experienced captain. The captain could do all that he can to re-assure the co-pilot, but they still may not share a common expectation of requirements for performance.

Leadership can be a powerful barrier, particularly if it is combined with other factors:

- 'New Guy' pilot
- 'Sky God' captain hero pilot
- 'timid co-pilot'
- 'go with the flow' pilot
- 'This is my first flight; I'll say something next time. I'm sure it'll be ok' pilot

Many accidents have occurred because a monitoring pilot just didn't speak up. Both pilotshave a part to play in ensuring that the authority gradient works. Good leadership and good followership go hand in hand.

Example

Read UK AAIB Accident Report 7/2008 – Aerospatiale SA365N in Morcambe Bay on 27 December 2006.[26]

The crew became spatially disoriented, but due to a lack of standard calls, PM monitoring and a sterile cockpit failed to successfully recognise and counter the spatial disorientation and successfully handing over control, leading to flight into water.

---

[26] https://www.gov.uk/aaib-reports/aar-7-2008-aerospatiale-sa365n-g-blun-27-december-2006

Positive Communication

Positive communication requires work on the part of both Captain and the Co-Pilot.

It does not mean that every communication is finished with words of praise and congratulation, but that pilots and crew members take steps to ensure that communication is rewarded and made a positive experience leading to increased cooperation through:

- Listen critically
- Request clarification by asking questions
- Presenting ideas in a way that shows respect
- Interacting in a supportive and constructive way
- Applying assertive strategies

Asserting Yourself

The helicopter cockpit can be a high-pressure, high-workload, noisy environment; because of this, it is important for a pilot to consider how they engage in a discussion and how various strategies to communicate can may affect crew co-operation and the ability to work together as a team.

When discussing problems or making observations, there are a number of approaches that can be used in trying to make our opinion heard.

Passive Behaviours

Passive Behaviour is when a pilot fails to stand up for themselves and allows others to override or ignore what they are saying. The pilot may be communicating in such a way that other people disregard their words or actions. Failure to honestly express feelings which may be to avoid conflict.

Assertive Behaviours

Assertive behaviour is when a pilot does stand up for themselves and others do listen to what is being said.

Standing up for yourself in a way that does not disregard the other person's opinion. Respects boundaries of all parties and results in fewer emotional outbursts. Assertiveness requires persistence, objectivity and validation to stay focussed on the issue and avoid becoming defensive or emotional. Assertiveness may also involve inquiry and advocacy.

Inquiry

Asking questions to acquire additional information.

Advocacy

The assertiveness of the individual in stating and defending a position.

Aggressive

Standing up for yourself but in a way that disregards the opinion of the other Demonstrated by the use of verbal and non-verbal cues such as defensive, superior statements, insincere or overblown descriptions of importance and a dominating posture. More aggressive behaviour may be required in a time-pressured situation, such as an emergency.

Intercom Protocols

Idle Conversation

It is not uncommon for there to be periods of less activity during flight, so the Flight Crew will be more inclined to have an open conversation that may not relate to the flight.

This is referred to as idle conversation, and this may be an important part of establishing a working relationship with your colleagues, and getting to know them; however, there will be times when this will not be appropriate, and a *sterile cockpit* policy will need to be used.

Sterile Cockpit definition

No flight crewmember may engage in, nor may any pilot in command permit, any activity during a critical phase of flight that could distract any flight crewmember from the performance of his or her duties or which could interfere in any way with the proper conduct of those duties.

Critical phases of flight include;

- From engine start to top of climb
- From top of descent until the aircraft has stopped at the completion of the flight
- During the handling of any abnormal or emergency situations
- Any operation below 500 ft AGL
- During any NVIS flight
- During any formation flight
- During any training sequences

In general, the term 'sterile cockpit' refers to the crew only communicating items relevant to the aircraft's operation.

Sterile cockpit use

Regulators introduced sterile cockpits in response to a number of aviation accidents where the investigation found that idle conversation and non-flight related discussions in the cockpit had caused or contributed to accidents by distracting a crew from performing their duties.

Airlines, Military Units and Commercial Companies conducting more complex operations such as NVG, IFR or low-level work often state in their SOPs when sterile cockpit procedures should apply. Crews must be willing to stop idle conversation regardless of where the conversation is to complete tasks efficiently.

If crews need to eat, drink, make phone calls, or make idle conversation, they should do so at the appropriate time and after gaining permission from the Captain and not during any critcal stages of the flight.

Managing Workloads

Cockpit workload

The ability to function well decreases with excessive stress.

In the helicopter cockpit, if, as a pilot, it becomes apparent that the workload is too high to safely complete priority tasks then steps should be taken (if possible) to reduce the workload to ensure safety.

> **Example**
>
> Consider a helicopter on firefighting operations and conducting water bombing. The FP is about to refill the bucket from a dam with tall surrounding trees.
>
> At the same time ATC calls on the radio, the Fire Service also calls on the radio and there is conflicting traffic while the visibility is reducing due to thick smoke. The Co-Pilot is trying to communicate the fuel state and the fuel pump warning light activates.
>
> Clearly the pilots are now experiencing a very high workload and they are struggling to communicate. In this instance the pilot should simply stop attempting to refill the water bucket and fly to an area that is less busy and then start addressing issues in order of priority. Both crew will be able to complete priority safety tasks and work sound CRM principles to see if the systems can be recovered to allow the task to continue, or to safety land the helicopter.

Multi-Crew Cooperation *for Helicopter Pilots*

Assisting in managing workload

As a crew member, it is acceptable to offer or ask for assistance to help in managing workloads.

It may be something important or something unimportant. The point is that assistance is required and the crew member needs to ask for or direct another crew member to do or assist in the task.

This assistance can be for controlling the aircraft, maintaining position or maintaining the required clearances from obstacles. It may be to direct or ask for assistance when troubleshooting aircraft systems or conducting normal checklists.

In a crew environment, the purpose of the other pilot or crew member is to share the operating load to ensure that together all crewmembers have ample spare capacity.

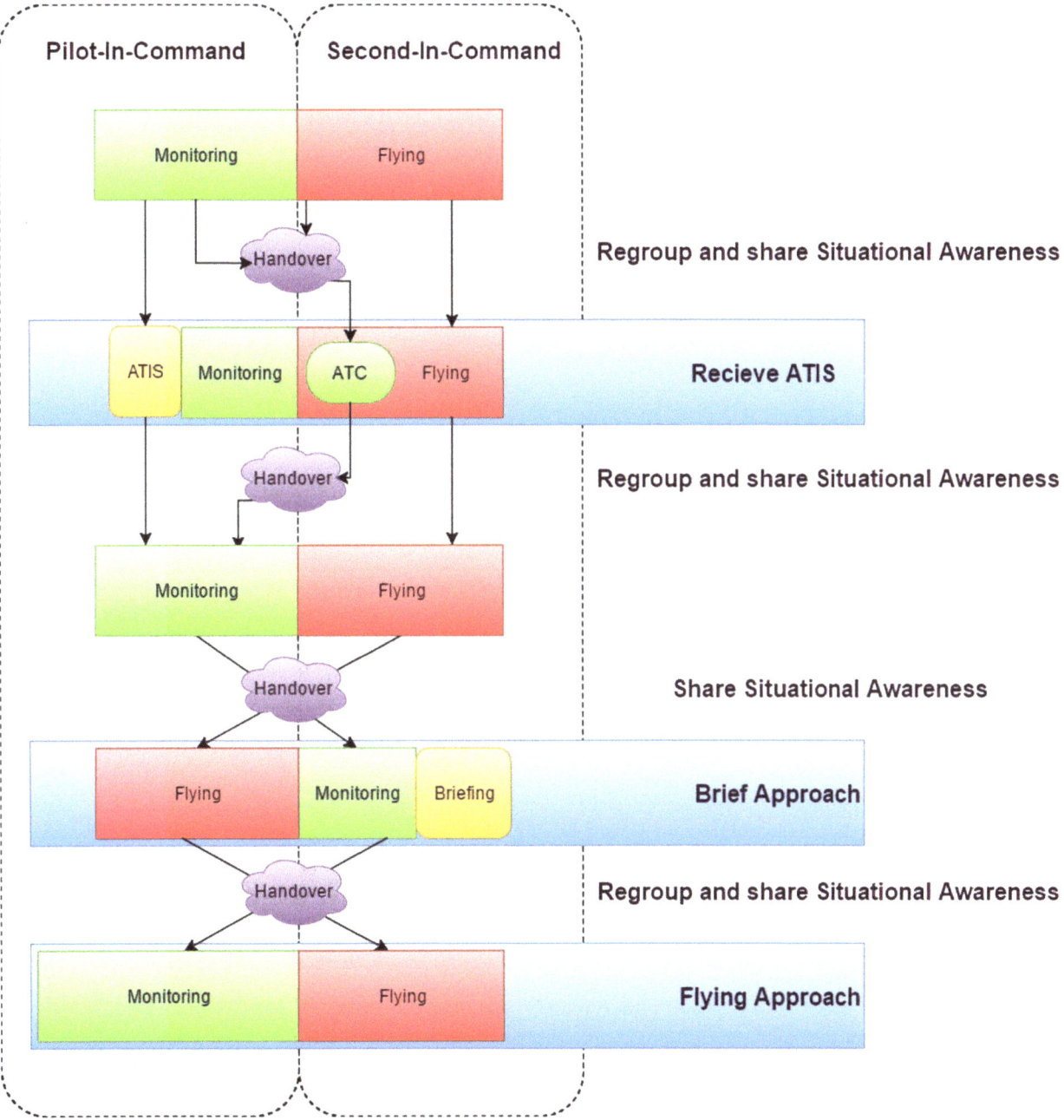

Example

Think about a helicopter beginning an instrument approach. The weather is bad and ATIS is changing frequently. Due to the poor weather, the radio is difficult to hear forcing the MP to concentrate entirely on listening to ensure that he copies it accurately.

Although the MP is usually responsible for the radios, in this case he is task saturated. You are the Co-pilot, and have control. Offer to take the ATC radios. It may be that the MP is so task saturated that he needs direction, in which case you may need to tell him *"You concentrate on getting the ATIS, my ATC radio comm 1"*. With time, you will gain experience in when it is appropriate to offer or direct, as either the SIC or PIC.

Remember to communicate. Once the PM has copied and briefed the ATIS take the time to regroup.

"Thanks Captain, Your ATC radios comm 2. Now cleared to descend to 1500 ft".

An important part of Multi-Crew operations is knowing when it is appropriate to diverge tasks, but taking the time to regroup.

Effective Leadership and Authority

General

In any MCC operation, crew coordination is vital to the safe and effective accomplishment of all flights.

The PIC has overall responsibility for the safety and success of the operation however this fact does not absolve the other crew members from their responsibility for doing all that is reasonable to improve safety and enhance the operation. An individual crew member's responsibility does not stop at the boundary of the job description for that position rather it extends to any area of the operation that the crew member comes in contact with.

Flying in a Multi-Crew environment is unquestionably a team effort. No single member is any less, or any more valuable than any other. During periods of high workload or high stress, it may be very difficult to ensure that critical information is assimilated and acted upon appropriately. It is the responsibility of the crew collectively and individually to ensure that critical information is passed, understood, and acted upon in a manner that fits the situation.

In a Multi-Crew environment, the purpose of the other pilot or crew member is to *share* the operating load. **Multi-Crew operations are not a competition to show-off to the other pilot how much you can do at once.** The real art of Multi-Crew operations is to manage the workload together to ensure that you both have ample spare capacity.

This can be a challenge to get right, and you must be aware of any cockpit authority gradient. You're not in training, you're operating. Act like a crew member, not a student.

No retribution

No crew member shall fear retribution for making an input with the intent of improving the operation.

No harassment

Harassment in any form in response to a crew member attempting to improve the operation will not be tolerated.

Pre-flight planning

Task assignment and maximisation of capacity begins during pre-flight preparation.

The ways that a crew work together before the flight set the tone for how they work together during the flight. With two people to share the jobs, the PIC uses the opportunity to gain 'head space' and ensure that all the key tasks are attended to.

Usually, pre-flight briefing will fall into a well practiced routine. For complex operations, there are opportunities to delegate tasks:

- Booking approaches and landings at other helipads and airfields
- Co-ordinating with SAR agencies
- Gathering the required in-flight publications
- Flight plan submission
- Obtaining weather and NOTAMS

However, there are some tasks that the PIC must personally ensure are completed:

- Review the helicopters maintenance records
- Reviewing relevant weather and NOTAMS
- Flight Planning
- Performance Calculations
- Weight and Balance Calculations
- Fuel calculations.

Even for simple missions, the availability of a second pilot provides the opportunity to discuss solutions to problems, cross-check calculations and ensure that capacity is increased and stress is reduced by effectively managing activities.

During pre-flight planning, build in periods for discussion and problem-solving. In particular for tasks where crew members may be split, ensure that you come back together to communicate and check for problems before the brief.

Ensure that before you begin the formal brief you've got answers to some key questions:

- Is everybody adequately rested?
- Is there anything that the PIC or SIC should be aware of?
- How will we co-ordinate key phases of the trip?
- What are our priorities for the sortie?

Briefing

In a multi-crew environment, briefings are the focal point of preparation and planning

The pre-flight brief is where the entire crew come together to ensure that all of the required pre-flight preparation is complete and that the crew share a common understanding of the task.

In general, the brief should not be the opportunity to bring up new problems and issues. A well-managed pre-flight preparation period should allow opportunities for discussion and problem-solving. When you get to the brief the aim is to have questions answered and conflicts resolved so that all crew members confirm understanding and leave with *shared situational awareness.*

A brief should conform to two main requirements:

- Structured
- Shared

The main points to be addressed during the brief don't differ too much from those covered during basic flight training. How is the weather, how are the NOTAMS, do we have enough fuel and is the trip authorised?

In general, for multi-crew operations, the briefing space and format is important:

We're a team in this together. **I am in charge.**

There is no single rule for how to conduct a brief, or how to participate in it. The PIC must be aware of the capabilities of the crew and the nature of the task. A complex, safety critical sortie with a less experienced crew may lend itself to a more formal briefing arrangement, as illustrated on the right to ensure that operations go 'by the book'.

A routine sortie where fatigue, team working and flight management are key, lends itself to a more relaxed approach on the left. Don't forget though that the PIC is still the leader. It is important that this fact is acknowledged and that the PIC is able to adjust the briefing style to suit the demands of the task. Whatever setting the PIC chooses, structure, leadership and followership are important.

Always finish with the opportunity to ask questions and check understanding.

Effectively Applying Standards

Flying in a Multi-crew environment can challenge any pilot when faced with the need to resolve poor group behaviours, external and internal pressures.

When we operate Multi-crew, we no longer just have to worry about ourselves. We also have to deal with a group dynamic. This can be particularly challenging if we find ourselves operating outside of the "Box Of Standards".

When operating as part of a crew, it can be tempting to let standards slip, particularly if you are used to working together, are good friends or if a more experienced pilot breaks SOP's to accomplish tasks faster, or to show off to a junior pilot.

The audio and report extract below is from a Puma crash in the UK in 2007. The subsequent enquiry found multiple breakdowns in CRM and adherence to checklists and SOP's that caused a fatal accident.

The pilots were operating as a crew, but were having a 'good time', rather than applying SOP to complete a job safely.

Puma Crash, UK, 2007

Audio:

https://www.youtube.com/watch?v=cdwKrzWU19g

Report:

https://www.gov.uk/government/publications/service-inquiry-into-the-into-puma-za934-helicopter-crash-at-catterick-on-8-august-2007

If you find yourself operating outside of the box of standards, think about why, correct the problem.

Multi-Crew Cooperation *for Helicopter Pilots*

Is there a pressure that has taken us outside of the box of standards? If so, take steps to resolve the pressure, do not operate in an area of higher risk unless it was known, planned for and authorised during the pre-flight brief.

If a crew member is operating outside of the box of standards, then the situation must be addressed. This can take courage and practice. All crew members can do their part to reduce conflicts by making a professional decision not to be the person who breaks the rules.

- Violating sterile cockpit procedures
- Taking shortcuts in checklists
- Ignoring SOP

Crew members should think about what might be done to deal with poor behaviours before they experience a real situation. Address the issue with the offender calmly and professionally. Explain that the crew are operating outside of the standards and should not do so.

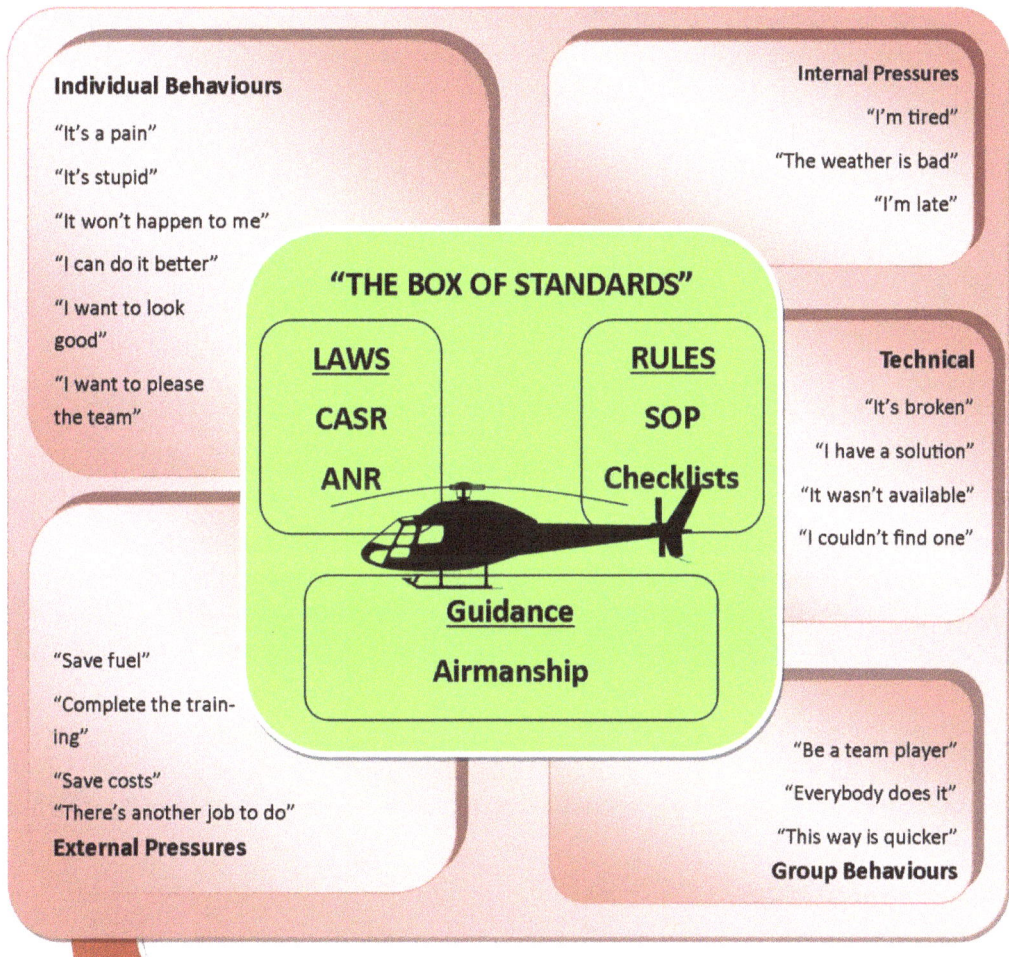

Actions outside the "Box of Standards" increase risk to you and your employer.

If you find yourself operating outside of the box of standards, think about why.

Can you identify a pressure that has taken you outside of the box of standards? If so, take steps to resolve the pressure, not allow it to make you operate in an area of higher risk.

If you find yourself routinely operating outside of the box of standards: Talk to your manager. Operations cannot be conducted outside of the law, and should only be conducted outside of established rules and guidance after careful planning. If you are routinely making decisions to push the rules too far, or if you find yourself breaking rules to complete tasks then either the rules should be changed (allowing the company to acknowledge the safety impacts), or the tasks must be modified.

You make a positive contribution to safety when you report and address operations outside of the box of standards.

If operations *routinely* take place outside of the box of standards: Talk to management. Operations cannot be conducted outside of the law and should only be conducted outside of established rules and guidance after careful planning. If decisions are routinely made to push the rules too far, or if rules are broken to complete tasks on behalf of the company then either the rules should be changed (allowing the company to know the safety impacts), or the tasks must be modified.

Pilots make a positive contribution to safety when they report and address operations outside of the box of standards.

Monitoring and Maintaining Performance

Monitoring crew performance.

Remember: Working in a Multi-crew environment means utilising shared capacity to accomplish tasks without any one individual becoming saturated, overloaded or losing SA.

The PM's job is to take care of routine tasks so that the PF can concentrate on flying safely and accurately. This takes practice, training and good communication skills from all crew members.

Pressures on performance:

- Fatigue
- Weather
- Instrument Scan
- Inexperience
- Fuel
- Radios

The PIC has ultimate responsibility for monitoring crew performance, but all crew members should be mindful of pressures that their colleagues face.

Primary performance pressures

Traditionally, the image of the PIC / SIC was of the mentor and the student. We now consider the relationship of two professionals. It is still tempting to think of the PIC as being responsible for monitoring the SIC in the PF or PM role, and vice versa but there may be other pressures that we assume are not there. It is the responsibility of the pilots to monitor each other during crew operations, not just of the PM to monitor the PF:

Routine monitoring and task allocation should be planned to allow one pilot, usually the PM, the 'capacity seat' with the capacity to monitor the PF. This works well for general flying tasks and allows the PF to concentrate on critical tasks while giving the PM the opportunity to manage routine processes and monitor the PF.

Secondary performance pressures

Operating on a Multi-Crew flight deck the crew should also be aware of the secondary pressures, and particularly those that might be hidden by the cockpit authority gradient. The PIC role brings additional pressures and responsibilities and the SIC is available to assist. An experienced SIC will still be an inexperienced PIC. Pilots operating multi-crew should be aware of these hidden pressures, and should not be afraid to acknowledge them during pre-flight briefings and in-flight if necessary.

Signs of performance breakdown

Signs of breakdown in performance can include:

- **Continual deviation from SOP**

    Deviating from SOP can also provide a pilot with indications that something is not right. A system is malfunctioning, external pressure which could cause an error exists, fatigue has set in, or a breakdown in CRM has occurred. If you or the other pilot are continually deviating from SOP, take a step back and think about why.

- **Loss of hearing**

    When people concentrate on a task it is usual for listening ability to be lost. This is one reason why intercom discipline and addressing your other crewmembers before speaking is important, but if you cannot get a response it may be that fatigue or overload has set in.

- **Inability to take in information**

    When somebody has become disoriented, they typically fail to understand new information. Signs that this is occurring can be frequently re-asking for information (like weather, or step heights) or not acknowledging important information.

- **Failure to prioritise tasks**

    Signs include becoming very directive, always saying "later", or "we'll do this first". The PIC has the right and authority to set task goals and the order of execution but when working together if inputs and suggestions are continually ignored it can be a sign that crew performance is breaking down.

Dealing with performance breakdown

If a pilot believes that an individual's performance is deteriorating then it should be immediately addressed. Positive, direct communication is the key. A subtle approach like "Are you OK" may work, but if a pilot has persevered into the position where their performance is deteriorating they will probably not have identified it and may not be willing or able to ask for help.

If in doubt, rationally identify the problem and suggest a course of action. Say "I think that we're getting task saturated here, let's take a step back and prioritise".

If disorientation has set in this can be very dangerous. If in doubt remember the emergency phrase "YOU MUST LISTEN".

Remember to exercise patience and focus when processing large amounts of data. If it is particularly important to deal with complex data (for example, when you need to re-plan a task while airborne) then it can be a good idea to take the decision to take time-out to concentrate on just that task. Build a plan to gain some time and then concentrate on the complex task until you have a satisfactory answer leaving the PF to deal with the aircraft for a moment. In the long run, the answer is more likely to be correct and it'll probably take less time.

When dealing with performance breakdown:

- Consider the condition (ability) of other crew members to perform crew duties;
- Monitor and appraise crew members' performance;
- Assist other crew members to manage workload;
- Motivate and support other crew members;
- Identify the signs, stages and possible causes of stress and conflict;
- Apply strategies to manage stress and conflict.

When to Intervene

When to intervene can be simple for a Captain but traditionally it is difficult for a Co-Piot. Traditionally the co-pilot is faced with a no win situation as they:

- Risk upsetting cockpit relationships by pointing out errors or
- Risk operating outside of known safe parameters by not pointing out errors.

To help resolve this basic dilemma the **P.A.C.E.R.** acronym is used to give each pilot the tools on when and how to intervene.

P.A.C.E.R.

The acronym **P.A.C.E.R.** defines the five steps in an ordered progression of inquiries designed to reduce risk at each level of the intervention sequence between the PM and the PF

P	Probe	Probe for a better understanding of what the other pilot is doing and thinking
A	Alert	Alert the pilot flying of the anomalies or the problem
C	Challenge	Challenge the suitability of the present strategy or flight configuration
E	Emergency	Emergency warning of critical and immediate dangers
R	Recover	Recover by intervening and taking over if necessary

Using the P.A.C.E.R. skills will enable any pilot to effectively intervene when another pilot (in particular the Captain or Flying Pilot) is not performing up to reasonable professional standards.

Consider the Pilot Monitoring (PM) advising the Pilot Flying (PF) that the speed is too low and the PF is not responding. The communication sequence may go as follows:

P	Probe	PM: "How is the approach speed low?"
A	Alert	PM: "Check speed. Target is 100 kt"
C	Challenge	PM: "You are slow, accelerate now to 100 kt"
E	Emergency	PM: "I am uncomfortable with the speed, go around"
R	Recover	PM: "Taking over, I have control, going around"

Another example may by a crew conducting low flying operations, the PM has seen a wire but the PF is not responding. The communication sequence may go as follows:

P	Probe	PM: *"Have you seen the poles and wire at 12 o'clock same level 2 miles?"*
A	Alert	PM: *"Caution we are approaching a wire 12 o'clock same level"*
C	Challenge	PM: *"You are on a collision course with a wire at 12 o'clock, you need to avoid it"*
E	Emergency	PM: *"I am not happy you need to turn now "*
R	Recover	PM: "Taking over, I have control"

Maintaining Situational Awareness

Situational awareness

The competencies for maintaining situational awareness include:

- actively monitoring flight path, aircraft configuration and systems to achieve desired performance using a systematic scan technique;
- advise pilot flying of deviations from planned operations;
- utilise available resources to collect flight environment information and modify planned operations when required;
- analyse aircraft systems and flight environment information to identify actual and potential threats or errors;
- cross-check the actions of other crew members.

The Awareness Test

https://www.youtube.com/watch?v=vJG698U2Mvo

Having another crew member allows us to counter channelized attention. When both are trained in CRM and HF we gain a safety system that can act to keep an overwatch of aircraft operations while one pilot concentrates on a demanding task and act to resolve scenarios where situational awareness could be lost, preventing accidents and incidents.

Ensuring Crew Members are aware of changes to systems

To ensure effective and well-coordinated actions in the aircraft, all crew members must be aware of the expected movements and unexpected individual actions. Each crew member will announce any actions that affect the actions of the other crew members.

> **Example**
>
> A helicopter is conducting fire-fighting operations and the FP is using a GPS waypoint to judge his distance from the drop point. While the FP is busy in the hover, ATC ask for a position report in relation to a nearby airfield so the PM enters a new waypoint into the GPS and passes the distance information on to ATC. The PM doesn't state to the PF that the GPS has been adjusted and because he was concentrating on a critical manoeuvre, the FP doesn't notice the change.
>
> Once the task is complete the PF maintains control but becomes spatially disoriented when his mental picture doesn't match the information on his flight display as the GPS is no longer referencing the drop point.

Make Effective Decisions

Identifying Problems

During CRM training, we were shown a number of techniques for decision making and problem solving:

- Identifying personal attitudes hazardous to safe flight.
- Learning behaviour modification techniques.
- Learning how to recognise and cope with stress.
- Developing risk assessment skills.
- Using all resources.
- Evaluating the effectiveness of one's decision-making skills.

Pilots must select a problem solving model that works for them, but each requires taking a structured approach to evidence gathering, analysis and decision making:

DECIDE

- **Detect:** Detection of changes
- **Estimate:** Estimate the need for counter measures or react to the change
- **Choose:** Choose a safe outcome
- **Identify:** Identification of actions which will successfully control the change
- **Do:** Implement the chosen actions
- **Evaluate:** Evaluate the effect of action in countering the change and progress of the flight.

GRADE

- **Gather –** Ensure that you have all the information that you need about the situation.
- **Review –** State the situation and ensure that everybody agrees.
- **Analyse –** Determine a suitable solution based on the information available
- **Decide –** State a decision and a plan of action. Remember that ultimately, the decision lies with the PIC, in particular if there are conflicting opinions.
- **Evaluate –** Don't be afraid to review the decision if circumstances change or you learn more about a situation.

Making decisions as a crew

Ultimately, Multi-crew operations has two goals:

- Manage workloads to improve safety margins.
- Make effective decisions by working as a team.

Aviation is, in its nature, a series of decisions. The nature of multi-crew operations brings two aspects to consider:

- The availability of additional resources to help in making decisions and managing workloads.
- The requirement to ensure that the whole crew maintain a working relationship and situational awareness.

Ultimately, this means that for a multi-crew operation to be successful, a consultative approach must be taken to decision making.

The information presented in this chapter is intended to give you the benefit of experience, hints and tips to allow you to make the best use of crew resources to allow success in both workload management and decision making. There are only a few simple guidelines that govern most decision making:

- The PIC maintains the authority to have the final say in resolving conflicts
  Note that this is "in resolving conflicts", not just "the final say". This is important, no matter how well a crew is working together as conflicts can, and will, arise due to lack of time and diffeences in mental picture.
- Lack of time can be countered through building in additional time or forward-planning.
- Differences in mental picture are resolved through a consultative approach and taking time to conduct thorough briefs to ensure a shared situational understanding.

Differences of opinion may still occur despite shared mental models and regardless of the time pressure (or lack of it). Ultimately, this is where the PIC will earn his money, for at the end of the day, it is he or she who carries the responsibility of command and the need to make a final decision.

Note though, that should an unresolvable difference of opinion occur, the following advice should be considered:

- If two courses of action are equally preferable, consider the opinion of the SIC and the option to try his or her idea, particularly if safety is not impacted.
- **Make a decision**, and clearly state that you are making a decision.
- If choosing a course of action that is not universally agreed, take time to explain to the crew why you are taking it, particularly explaining the reasons for not selecting the alternatives.
- Once the decision is made, do not allow conflict to continue. Immediately remember your CRM and team working techniques to ensure that the crew work together towards the selected plan.
- If you are not the PIC, exercise good followership and ensure that the task is completed and that CRM continues at the highest standards
- Make sure you discuss the issue in detail during debrief. Focus on improving the performance for next time, learning from the issue and achieving an optimum outcome next time.
- Do not be afraid to change your mind, or select an alternative plan, if the situation changes or it becomes clear that the selected course of action is not the best. Continue to apply the **DECIDE** or **GRADE** loop.

Resource Allocation

Successful leadership and resource allocation

The example below represents successful leadership and resource allocation.

Example

Jane and Bob are conducting a fire spotting task at night using NVG's. They receive a message from ATC that a light aircraft has gone missing after transmitting a MAYDAY and they have confirmation that their operations center has authorised them to take part in Search operations.

The location is only ten minutes flight time away. The crew could transit there at low level and they are not fatigued, but the terrain in the area is different and fuel is a concern. There are some closer airfields that the crew could use for a refuel later in the night but they had only planned for a simple operation to and from their main operating base.

Bob realises that he has a complex plan to complete to ensure that they can get maximum time on the search and can operate safely in the new area. He also knows that he'll be operating under NVG's in an area that he isn't familiar with and that wasn't briefed before the flight. Bob has conducted Search and Rescue before, he therefore breaks down the job of searching for the aircraft into tasks:

1. Crew safety
2. Transit
3. Fuel & Planning
4. Safety briefing
5. Task briefing
6. Conducting the task

Bob prioritises his tasks co-ordinating with Jane. First he ensures that the crew will remain safe. They climb above safety altitude and Bob obtains clearance from ATC to the search area and checking the aircraft systems. He knows that he needs some time to safely plan and so asks Jane to lower the IAS. Once the aircraft is in level flight and Bob is happy that Jane has full situational awareness Bob briefs her that he will be isolating himself from radios and concentrating just on the planning task and that Jane is in charge of flying the aircraft and operating the Radios under NVFR with NVG's.

> **Example**
>
> Jane acknowledges this and Bob then removes his goggles and turns on his finger light to start planning. In three minutes Bob has completed a thorough plan, has fuel for three possible landing airfields calculated as well as a full brief for the crew on the new operating area, wire hazards, terrain, safety altitudes and low-level radio frequencies.
>
> Having completed this task he addresses Jane and first checks that they have shared Situational awareness. He asks her what has changed, she replies that ATC passed weather and a lowest forecast pressure for the area and briefs Bob. Bob then conducts a full brief on the new operating area and fuel plan, including giving Jane the opportunity to consider and challenge. He then changes his tone and gives Jane some direction – she hasn't done anything like this before and so Bob clearly gives her roles concentrating on aircraft safety.
>
> One the brief is complete Bob turns off the cabin lights, replaces his NVG and the crew re-commence NVG operations. By effectively prioritising tasks, using his crew and exercising good CRM a thorough plan is conducted in considerably less time than it would have taken if Bob was concentrating on radios and monitoring Jane. The crew was able to balance immediate risks to ensure a safe course of action that meant they had a full plan to safely conduct the search, that the whole crew agree to and that maintains their situational awareness.
>
> He did this by:
>
> - Allocating resources and time.
> - Breaking down the overall task (search for a lost aircraft) into subtasks
> - Maintaining focus when processing information
> - Managed time and resources to ensure work was completed safety and effectively
> - Ensured that responsibility for flight path management was assigned
> - Exercising effective leadership and authority

Preparation for Practical Lessons

Single pilot operations

Traditionally when a pilot first learns to fly they do so as a "single pilot."

This means that the pilot learns how to manage the aircraft under normal, abnormal and emergency conditions by themselves. They make all the decisions and do all of the work. They also shoulder all of the responsibility.

With the modernisation of aircraft comes much more sophistication and automation which can also lead to more complex tasks (IFR, NVG, SAR EMS etc).

There are more systems to manage and there is a greater demand to manage external traffic and communications, which means the single pilot can get very busy in the cockpit which can lead to a reduction in safety.

Commercial airlines

In the fixed wing world, all commercial airlines operate with a minimum of two (2) pilots in the cockpit with the majority of the airline aircraft **certified** by the manufacturer to only be operated by a minimum of two (2) pilots.

Military operations

In the military world it is also normal procedure to have a minimum two (2) pilot crew so each can continually be checking and supporting the other.

Often in the military, MCC also can include the overall commander, weapons and airspace co-ordination officers and even the Aircrewman.

Multi-crew certified helicopters

In the civil helicopter world it has typically been common for helicopters to be operated by a single pilot, however, it is quickly becoming more common for new, larger helicopters to also now be **certified** by the manufacturer to be operated by a minimum of two (2) pilots.

In a helicopter that is **certified** by the manufacturer to operate with a minimum two (2) pilot crew then the most senior pilot shall hold an Airline Transport Pilot Licence (ATPL) but both pilots shall be trained and certified in MCC operations.

Preferred Multi-crew operations

Notwithstanding the above, the helicopter does not have to be certified by the manufacturer as a multi-crew aircraft for the operator to **choose** to operate it with two (2) pilots instead of one (1).

Many Helicopter Operators now prefer the use of a two (2) pilot crew in high workload operations such as IFR, NVG, Search and Rescue and offshore transfers.

This means there is a requirement to train the qualified "single pilots" how to operate as part of a team in the cockpit so that the two (2) pilots together, can manage normal, abnormal and emergency operations together.

MCC Training

Multi-crew Cooperation (MCC) training is designed to manage the Human Factor issues in the multi-crew cockpit environment.

MCC training is a pre-requisite to a Multi-crew Pilot Licence (MPL) and an Airline Transport Pilot Licence (ATPL). It is also a pre-requisite for any grade of licence where the pilot will be performing duties within the cockpit as part of a multi-crew operation.

Differences

Because the fixed wing airline business represents the vast majority of flying with two (2) crew in the cockpit, all the rules around Multi-Crew Cooperation have been developed with this in mind.

Airlines typically follow very predictable paths and do very predictable things which in itself helps in the operation being much safer. However, the helicopter world does not operate in the same manner, so the way we go about operating a helicopter, particularly as a multi-crew can be vastly different.

This means helicopter pilots really need to be conducting helicopter specific MCC training to account for the differences in the way we operate rather than completing a MCC course in say a Boeing 737 fixed wing simulator.

Example

Consider the differences in an airliner flying from Sydney to Auckland under the IFR in a Multi-crew environment compared to a Rescue Helicopter tasked on a search in the Bass Straight using NVGs.

Both crews require MCC training and both need to function as a high level team, but the demands and operational complexities of each operation are worlds apart.

Pre-requisites

As a pre-requisite to commencing specific MCC training on a specific aircraft type it is important that each crew member has had some training in:

- Human Factors
- Aeromedical Factors
- Risk Management
- Threat Error Management and
- Crew Resource Management

The basic knowledge for this would have been covered in the CPL, ATPL or Military equivalent Human Factors theory course as well as additional expanded revision material provided in this MCC for Helicopter Pilots reference material.

Standard Operating Procedures (SOPs)

Standard Operating Procedures are produced by the Company or Military Unit and contain descriptive detail on how each stage of flight is to be conducted and how flight crew members are to function within a Multi-crew environment in a particular type of aircraft.

SOPs are usually Company or Military Unit specific based on the configuration and operation of a particular aircraft type. This means that different Company or Military Units may have different SOPs for the same aircraft.

What to Standardise

When operating as part of a multi-crew the following items should be standardised through the use of an SOP.

Phraseology

The way in which words and phrases are used in a pre-determined format to have a specific meaning within the cockpit.

Many standard words and phrases have already been explained under the CRM portion of this course that are applicable to the entire aircrew, however additional words and phrases specific to MCC operations will be explained later in the MCC Standard words and phrases section.

Checklists

A check is a series of actions required to ensure the sequential and safe completion of a specific task.

A checklist is a combination of all the individual checks required to ensure the sequential and safe completion of a group of related tasks.

A checklist is most commonly a paper based document that remains in the aircraft and is formatted in a manner that allows efficient flow, in a logical sequence to maintain the safety of the aircraft. In modern helicopters the checklist may be electronic.

The way in which checklists are carried out should always be standardised within an organisation.

Drill

A drill is a series of checks required to be conducted during an abnormal or emergency situation that requires immediate action and is therefore, carried out from memory without reference to the checklist.

The way in which drills are carried out, and the extent to which actions must be memorised is governed by SOP.

Challenge / Response

The Challenge and Response method allows for two pilots to work together to cross-check aircraft configurations and flight operations with each other.

One pilot will state the "*Challenge*," this is an item on the checklist that requires an action, decision or confirmation while the other pilot performs the appropriate action and then "*Responds*" to the challenge once successfully completing the check by verbally stating what the action was.

Example	
Challenge	*Response*
"Battery"	Selects the battery to the ON position and then verbally states: *"ON"*

If the responder does not provide the required response, the checklist reader should pause, state the response required and the responder should then re-confirm that the correct checklist action has been carried out before stating the required response.

Identify / Confirm / Select

When the PF or PM need to move a particular switch, lever, knob or similar then there will be times when this needs to be articulated (spoken out loud) and then confirmed by the other pilot before it is actually moved.

In general, under normal conditions any item listed on the Normal or Abbreviated Checklist requiring the pilot to move the switch, lever, knob or similar can do so without articulating this procedure. Instead it can be said in their head as a mantra so that nothing is simply done automatically. This is referred to as a self-check using the "identify / confirm / select" method.

The other pilot should monitor selections and correct the pilot carrying out the checklist item if a mistake is made, or is about to be made.

If, in an emergency situation, and using the Emergency Checklist where the particular switch, lever, knob or similar is going to affect a flight control, engine configuration or fuel, then, it must be articulated and confirmed by the other pilot prior to being moved. This is to ensure that in an emergency no incorrect movement of switches, levers, knobs or similar are made that could potentially make the situation worse.

Consider flying a twin engine helicopter and suffering an engine failure. If the Pilot Flying then shut down the good engine by mistake, this would make the emergency situation worse.

The pilot tasked to make the selection will first identify the correct switch, lever, knob or similar by placing his/her hand or finger on it.

The second pilot will then take the time to visually confirm that the correct switch, lever knob or similar has been identified by the first pilot, that the first pilot's hand is on the correct item and then state "confirmed".

At that point the pilot making the selection will move the switch, lever, knob or similar while verbalising the checklist action.

Example

If a Hot Start occurs, the Multi-Crew actions for the IGN ENG CB would be as follows:

- PM – Place finger on CB, state
    "Confirm IGN ENG CB"
- PF – look, check and if the PM's finger is on the ING ENG CB, state
    "Confirmed"
- PM – Pull CB and state
    "Out"

The most important point for the PF is to actually look and check that the correct switch is selected. If the PM has his finger on the wrong switch, state clearly:

"Negative, that is the wrong switch"

MCC Roles and Responsibilities

What needs to be defined

The allocation of roles and responsibilities should be documented by the Company or Military Unit as Standard Operating Procedures (SOPs) and should clearly identify:

- Who is in charge whilst on the ground?
- Who conducts the flight planning?
- Who conducts the pre-flight inspection?
- Who is responsible for the loading of fuel?
- Who is responsible for loading the payload and calculating the weight and balance?

- Who is in charge whilst in the air?
- Who conducts what actions during the different phases of flight including:
- the start, run-up, lift-off and taxi?
- the departure, climb, cruise and descent?
- the approach, termination, taxi and landing?
- the shutdown and after flight checks?
- How the PM calls out the checklist items, the "*Challenge*", and how the PF carries out the check and then "*Responds*" to the challenge.
- Who is responsible for which actions in the event of an emergency?
- Who is responsible for what when a threat or an error is identified?
- How is the scan conducted in a multi-crew?
- How is the handover-takeover procedure conducted?
- What happens if one of the crew is incapacitated or unfit for duty?
- What duties may be delegated and by who to who?

FP / PM Roles

Throughout all phases flight, the PM shall be responsible for managing checklists.

The PM shall:

- Ensure that the required responses are provided
- Pause or mark for later auctioning, any checklist items that cannot be completed
- State on completion of a checklist "Checklist name, Complete"

No	Phase	Task	PM Role	PF Role
1	Start	In accordance with the checklist	Manage Checklists Provide checklist responses as required	Provide briefings Provide checklist responses as required
2	Departure	In accordance with the checklist	Challenge	Response
3	Climb	In accordance with the checklist	Challenge	Response
4	Cruise	In accordance with the checklist	Challenge	Response
5	Descent	In accordance with the checklist	Challenge	Response
6	Approach and termination	In accordance with the checklist	Challenge	Response
7	Taxi and Landing	In accordance with the checklist	Challenge	Response
8	Shut down	In accordance with the checklist	Challenge	Response
9	Abnormal and Emergency	In accordance with the checklist	Challenge	Response

PF / PM Responsibilities

Overview

Each role on an MCC flight will have defined responsibilities that must be carried out.

In general, these responsibilities may be made explicit through SOP's that state the ways in which the responsibility must be carried out.

Non-executive responsibilities can be delegated during the flight based on the workload of each crew member. If a responsibility is delegated it is important that whichever crew member it is assigned to, carries it out in accordance with any SOP's that exist for that responsibility.

The PF responsibilities

The Pilot Flying (PF) is responsible for operating the flight controls directly or through the autopilot in order to safely manoeuvre the helicopter as required, avoiding obstacles and accurately maintaining a HDG Altitude and speed within the helicopters limitations as required or directed by the PM.

The PF shall:

- Manage the control and configuration of the helicopter
- Maintain a constant lookout
- Monitor the helicopters limitations and power settings
- Communicate with the PM
- Take immediate actions in an emergency by memory
- "Respond" to all challenges by the PM
- Call for the commencement of a checklist
- Monitor the PM

The PM responsibilities

The Pilot Monitoring is responsible for advising the PF and taking care of all administrative tasks.

The PM shall:

- Communicate with the PF
- Monitor the PF
- Advise the PF if an aircraft or engine limitation is being approached
- Manage the navigation of the helicopter
- Manage the external radio calls to ATC and other aircraft
- Manage the checklist items and offer up a "Challenge" to the PF
- Call for the commencement of a checklist if it has not been requested by the PF
- Administer the checklist in an emergency
- When able assist in the lookout

MCC Checklists

The checklist is probably the single most important tool that is utilised within the Multi-crew cockpit. Following this approved sequential list of actions allows for the safe operation of the aircraft by using proven and tested methodologies.

In large aircraft on set routes, use of the checklist, in most cases, guarantees that all applicable items and scenarios are catered for.

In smaller aircraft or on routes that are not planned, often crews have to manage the checklists to only use those portions that are relevant.

Understanding checklist conventions, understanding how to read the checklist, knowing the words and phrases within the checklist and how to apply them is all part of being a professional aviator.

Range of checklists

Becker Helicopters provides a series of checklists for each of its aircraft types.

These checklists have been designed so they can be used for both:

- Single-crew or
- Multi-crew

The following checklists have been prepared based on the standardised Bell 206B3 helicopter used at Becker Helicopters.

- B206BIII Abbreviated Normal Procedures Checklist
- B206BIII Expanded Normal Procedures Checklist
- B206BIII Abbreviated Emergencies and Malfunctions Checklist
- Planning Checklist
- B206BIII Equipment Quick Reference Guide

Also available for reference are the:

- B206BIII Technical Manual, and
- B206BIII Training Rotorcraft Flight Manual (an uncontrolled copy of the Bell 206BIII Rotorcraft Flight Manual – used for training purposes only).

MCC SOPs

When conducting Multi-Crew operations at Becker Helicopters an additional **B206BIII MCC Standard Operating Procedures (SOPs)** booklet is provided.

This specifically details the procedures and standards for operating as a multi-crew in the B206BIII and is readily available to the crew in the cockpit.

The SOPs are designed to explain how to use the other checklists listed above in a multi-crew environment and the SOPs in applying that checklist in a multi-crew operation at Becker Helicopters.

Much of the information in this MCC chapter is repeated and abbreviated in the Becker Helicopters Operations Manual and the B206BIII MCC Standard Operating Procedures booklet.

Using the Checklist

Conventions

Each operator will have their own conventions for preparing checklists.

These conventions are driven by the types of operations, the complexity of the aircraft and guidelines of the relevant regulatory authority therefore it is important that each pilot receives standardisation and familiarisation training with each Company they work for.

This course will focus on the checklists used by Becker Helicopters in the Bell206BIII.

At Becker Helicopters

The checklists used at Becker Helicopters are designed to be flexible. We aim to design checklists that:

- Can be used for a wide range of operations including air transport, training, and aerial work
- Are suitable for less complex aircraft such as the Bell 206BIII
- Are flexible enough to be used either single-crew or multi-crew
- Are flexible enough to be used:
    - Day VFR
    - Night VFR
    - NVG; and/or
    - IFR
    - in an electronic format

Other operators

Other operators may have checklists that are designed specifically for:

- Only air transport operations
- Only IFR operations
- Only multi-crew operations

For example:

Consider a checklist for a Boeing 737 for Qantas, flying set routes under the IFR at high altitudes only, will look different when compared to a checklist that is designed for a Bell206BIII for Becker Helicopters flying no set routes, with varying operational requirements under the VFR, IFR and NVG at low altitudes.

Responsibility

When conducting checklists, the PM is responsible for managing the checklist. This is sometimes known as 'running' a checklist.

This means:

- Reading checks
- Conducting the required responses or ensuring that the PF responds correctly
- Correcting mistakes
- Tracking incomplete items, or pausing checklists until items can be complete
- Confirming that the checklist is complete once all items are finished

Challenge / Response Method

When using checklists in a multi-crew environment, the *"Challenge / Response"* method is used where:

- the Pilot Monitoring will state the *"Challenge,"* this is the item that requires checking, and
- the Flying Pilot will perform the appropriate check and then *"Respond"* to the challenge by verbally acknowledging once successfully completing the check.

Identify / Confirm / Select Method

The Identify / Confirm / Select Method is only required when using the Emergency Checklist where it affects a flight control, engine configuration or fuel.

It is not required when using the Normal or Abbreviated Checklist, However, it is good airmanship to silently use the Identify/Confirm/Select method as a self-check prior to moving a particular switch, knob, lever or control.

Checklist Discipline

Checklists exist to ensure that the aircraft is in the correct configuration for flight and operations, and to allow a crew to work in a structured manner to control against mistakes or solve problems.

During multi-crew operations, checklist discipline is important. Pilots and crew must have mastered all company SOP's and be familiar with the checklist to work efficiently in a crew.

When running a checklist, the reader must wait to hear the appropriate, published response before moving on to the next checklist item. Company SOP, common sense or good communication may dictate that some additional description is important. For example, talking about a limit, or stating a hydraulic pressure. However, the checklist action must always end with the pilot(s) or crew member(s) responsible for completing the check stating the appropriate "pro-word".

Example:

During dispatch checks, a crew may be responsible for checking that doors, hatches and harnesses are secure. The checklist contains the following item:

Hatches………………..Secure

In order to carry out the check, the company SOP is that crews conduct a verbal check of hatch position. Saying as they go "Check left, check right". This communication is important to ensure that the pilot or crew member carries out the check correctly every time, and to let the other pilot know that a key check is being done correctly. However, once the check has been completed the pilot should state "Secure" to confirm that the actions have been carried out.

This makes checklists more manageable. Imagine if every checklist for multi-crew operations contained every piece of information that had to be conveyed during a check – they would be unmanageable. However, the key point is that the pro-word must be delivered as written to confirm that the underlying checks have been completed.

If, as a checklist reader, you don't hear the required response, gently prompt for it if you know that the checks have been completed.

Example

PM: *"Hatches"*
  PF: *"Secure left, Secure Right........"*
PM: *"Confirm secure?"*
  PF: *"Secure".*

Always carry out the required check before stating the pro-word. Beware of the habit of stating the required response before checking the reading or selecting the service. Say what you see, not what you expect to see.

Checklist Conventions

Checklists will often have standard conventions used when preparing them.

For example, Becker Helicopters uses:

- Left and Right layout for checklists where the item on the left represents the "*Challenge*," and the statement on the Right represents the appropriate "*Response*"
- This may be demonstrated by the headings in the checklist having multiple meanings

For example:

The ***Item*** on the ***left*** can be referred to as the ***challenge*** by the ***PM***

The ***Action*** on the ***right*** can be referred to as the ***response*** by the ***PF***

Avionics Checks		
1. Helisas Autopilot:		
a. Cyclic Force Trim Button	P	Press 2 Seconds *(SAS light green)*
b. Force trim position	P	Tested
c. Force trim reset	P	Tested
d. Autopilot release button	P	Pressed *(SAS light white)*
e. Cyclic Force Trim Button	PM	Press 2 seconds *(SAS light green)*
f. Autopilot release button	PM	Pressed *(SAS light white)*
2. GPS:		
a. GPS database	PM	Checked
b. CDI Test	PM	Complete
3. Comm 1 & Comm 2	PM	Selected, briefed
4. ATIS	PM	Checked
5. Navaids:		
a. GPS	PM	Set *(flight plan / Waypoint checked)*
b. VOR / Standby / VLOC	PM	Tuned, identified, tested, set
c. NDB / Standby	PM	Tuned, identified, tested, set
d. Course Bar	PM	Set
6. Flight Instruments:		
a. Attitude Indicators	PM	Checked *(Flags clear)*
b. Altimeters	P,PM	Set, checked
c. Altitude Alert & Decision Altitude	P,PM	Set
d. Hdg Bug	P	Set *(Runway)*
e. Radalts	PM	Set as required
f. Flight Compass	P	Checked, Aligned +/- 10°
g. MFD	P	Reversionary on / X-Fill
7. Transponder	PM	Standby

Symbols may be used identify when different rules apply to steps on the checklist. A triangle may indicate the items required for a quick start or a square may indicate those items only required for night operations.

| 1 | ▲ | Quick start and abbreviated checklists for multiple flights and circuits. |
| 2 | ◾ | Required for NUA (NVFR) IFR and NVG operations.
(Representing the moon against the night sky). |

Checklist Response

Response only after completing action

The PF being challenged should only respond after completing the required check, action or confirmation and correcting any deviations from the correct settings if required.

Waiting for a response

The PM, should always wait for a definitive response from the PF and should cross-check the validity of the response (using the Identify/Confirm/Select method), as required before moving to the next item

Unexpected configuration

If achieving the required configuration according to the item "Challenged" is not possible, the PF should clearly and completely respond by stating the actual configuration. This could lead to the PF and PM conferring with each other and changing the plan.

Example

Consider the PM asking for the Landing Light to be turned ON for an approach to an unlit HLS but it is not working. Although the expected response should be the PF turning the Landing Light on and Responding with "*ON*" in this case it is not possible. The flow of the conversation may then be as follows:

> *PM: "Landing Light"*
>> *PF: "Landing Light Failed"*

Following this the two pilots may have to discuss another course of action and look at an alternative option. In the short term this may require a Go-Around and then some trouble shooting. It may also require the crew to consult an emergency checklist for an alternative action.

For example:

> *PF "Going around"*

The PIC would then initiate the discussion and alternatives and ask for suggestions from the crew. Some possible solutions may include:

> *"Consult the emergency checklist " (if applicable)*
> *"Check the circuit breaker"*
> *"Retry the switch"*
> *"Do we have an alternate source of light?"*
> *"Shall we divert back to base?" etc*

Completing a Checklist

Once a checklist or a specific section of the checklist has been completed the PM should mark the completion of the checklist by stating "(Checklist name) checklist complete." This will signify to both pilots that the start checklist has been completed and that next section of checklist may be commenced when applicable.

> **Example**

The Start Checklist has been completed. The PM would state:

> *"Start Checklist complete"*

The beginning of each section of a checklist is normally segregated by a bold heading or a line to indicate the end of one section and the beginning of another.

R	6.	Risks	P,PM	Threats, Errors briefed
	7.	Radios & Radiation		
		h. Comm 1, Comm 2	PM	Calls made
	8.	Transponder	PM	Set
	9.	RPM	P	100% Set

AFTER LANDING CHECKS

1.	Strobe lights	PM	Off
2.	Pitot Heat	CP	Off
3.	Search & Landing Lights	P	As required
4.	Transponder	PM	Standby
5.	Radios	PM	Call made *(runway vacated)*
6.	Engine Anti-Ice	CP	Off

Interrupted checklist

If for some reason it is necessary to interrupt a check, drill or procedure, then the PM giving the Challenge or the PF about to do the Action prior to giving a Response shall indicate the item that the check is being held at by stating "Holding at (item)."

> **Example**

Consider the requirement to talk to ATC during a Start Checklist. The PM may have to respond to ATC and temporarily stop the checklist. The PM will state:

> *PM: "Holding at position lights"*

Lost place in a checklist

Should the crew lose track of their progress through the checklist then the checklist section currently being used must be re-started from the beginning or in the best case scenario, commenced from the last item known to have been completed.

Completion of checks

All checks once started shall be carried out in the sequence that they are listed until complete. Company SOP may make it permissible to declare that an individual item is "to go" (for example, setting an altimeter), but may dictate that checklist items must be carried out in order, and the checklist should be held until an item can be completed.

Memorising checklists

Generally, the only checks, drills or procedures completed by memory are for emergencies that require immediate action; and checks that are typically done in a high workload environment where a memory procedure would be advantageous.

Memorising checklists is common in helicopter operations as the time available to consult a checklist is much less when compared to a fixed wing.

In multi-crew training, the checklist will be extensively used. As crews become very familiar with the content then certain checks may be done from memory at the discretion of the PIC and the demands of the operation.

Multi-Crew Cooperation *for Helicopter Pilots*

> **Example**
>
> When conducting a confined area in a helicopter, the PSWATP is often done by memory.
>
> In the beginning a checklist may be consulted but as the pilot gains experience and familiarity with the PSWATP format the checklist may not have to be consulted.
>
> This does not take away the requirement for the crew to be verbalising the check where the PM will challenge with "*Power*" and the PF will Respond with an answer such as "*Cat 3*" or "*100%*" etc.

Checklist Verbal Procedures

When "Challenging" or "*Responding*" use the specific wording detailed in the checklist. Do not try to abbreviate it or use a similar word as it may have a different meaning.

Whenever a specific quantity is involved, that quantity shall be stated in the response, For example:

"Speed 60 kt" or "Altitude 5300 feet"

When more than one crew member is required to respond, the standard sequence shall be: PF responds first then the PM second followed by any other crewmembers, if applicable.

> **Example**
>
> Consider a check where the PM has asked the crew to check their harnesses. All crew members are then required to respond. The sequence may be completed as follows:
>
> *PM challenge: "Harnesses secure"*
> *PF response: "Set right"*
> *PM response: "Set left"*
> *Additional crew in the back "Set left rear"*

When not to verbalise checklists

Checklists are normally carried out verbally. This is to further the Situational Awareness (SA) of and to provide a measure of monitoring and cross checking by other crew members. It helps the entire crew to have the same "mental model" of the operation.

Situations may arise where it is more desirable to silently carry out a specific check, drill or procedure that is normally done verbally. This may be due to a high workload in the cockpit where ATC and other requirements are providing a distraction and there is busy radio chatter.

In such a situation the PIC may direct that a specific check, drill or procedure be carried out silently. The applicable crew member will then verbally state only when the check is complete.

> **Example**
>
> Consider a routine CLEAROFF check. At top of climb it is important to action together to ensure that both pilots share common SA. However, during a long transit in a busy ATC environment it may be unnecessarily disruptive to action the routine CLEAROFF checks as challenge-response. SOPs, therefore, allows the PM to carry out a routine CLEAROFF check silently and just to inform the PF when it is completed.

Checklist on the ground

All checklists performed on the ground are *initiated* at the command of the **PIC**

Example

If wanting to commence the start checklist the PIC will state "*Starting Checklist*"

The checklist will then be conducted between the PF and PM in the normal manner.

Checklists in flight

All checklists performed in flight are *initiated* at the command of the **Pilot Flying (PF)**. The PIC, however, still retains final authority for all actions directed or performed.

Example

Consider a hydraulic failure in flight.

The PF will fly the helicopter and announce the problem. After establishing control of the helicopter the PF will then request that the PM complete the emergency checklist items.

> PF "*Hydraulic failure. Maintaining 1000ft HDG 260 reducing speed to 60 -70kts. Your checklist items*"

The designated PM will then act as the "*Challenger*" and the PF the "*Responder*" in the normal manner.

At the completion of the emergency checklist, if there is an executive decision to make then it shall be made by the PIC.

Example

Consider when after completing the emergency checklist for a hydraulic failure it is determined that it cannot be rectified, it will be the PIC who makes the decision to land, divert or continue.

Initiating checklists

If the PF fails to initiate a normal checklist, good Crew Resource Management (CRM) practice dictates that the PM should compensate by suggesting the initiation of the checklist.

Example

Consider the requirement to commence a descent for an instrument approach and the PF has not asked for the Descent checks to be completed. The PM shall speak up as follows

> PM: "*Ready for Descent checks?*"
> PF: "*Yes - Descent checks*"

Normal checklists should be called in a timely manner during low-workload periods (conditions permitting) to prevent any undue time pressure or possible interruption that could defeat the purpose of the checklist and potentially be detrimental to safety.

Time and workload management, including the availability of the other pilot to participate, are key factors in the initiation and effective conduct of normal checklists.

MCC Standard Words and Phrases

The use of standard words and phrases can be divided into two (2) categories.

1. Those words and phrases that are used throughout normal flight which have already been covered in the CRM section of the course, and
2. Those words and phrases that may be used by the crew to alert other crew members to undesired conditions or abnormal flight. These words and phrases typically are short and are not necessarily designed to tell the other pilot what to do. Instead the word or phrase is a prompt or a notification to other pilot.

Escalation

In "When to intervene" you were introduced to the "PACER" method of escalation.

- Probe
- Alert
- Challenge
- Emergency Warning
- Recover

The table below provides standard words and phrases to be used in the 'Alert' phase.

They are designed to aid the Flight Crew to better communicate and be aware of something and that an action or response is required. The PF should be able to identify exactly what needs correcting and do it without further input from the PM.

Item	Call	Description
Abnormal Bank	"Bank" or "Angle of Bank"	Upon observing an abnormal Angle of Bank the PM should call: *"Bank"* or *"Angle of Bank"* The PF should respond with: *"Roger, correcting"* and correct the bank to less than 30° angle of bank or if the excess angle of bank is necessary, call: *"Roger intentional"*
Abnormal Rate of Descent	**Rate of Descent**	Upon observing an abnormal Rate of Descent the PM should call: *"Rate of Descent"* The PF should respond with: *"Roger, correcting"* and reduce the rate of descent to within normal parameters or if the abnormal rate is necessary, call: *"Roger, intentional"* and continue.

Item	Call	Description
Abnormal Rate of Climb	**Rate of Climb**	Upon observing an abnormal Rate of Climb the PM should call: *"Rate of Climb"* The PF should respond with: *"Roger, correcting"* and reduce the rate of climb to within normal parameters **or** if the abnormal rate is necessary, call: *"Roger, intentional"* and continue.
Abnormal Speed	**Speed**	Upon observing an abnormal Speed the PM should call: *"Speed"* The PF should respond with: *"Roger, correcting"* and correct the speed to within the normal parameters, **or** if the abnormal speed is necessary, call: *"Roger intentional"* and continue.
Climb Power	**Climb Power**	To command the setting of Climb Power either pilot may call: *"Set Climb Power"* The PF should then set Climb Power as specified in the Flight Manual and respond with: *"Roger, set climb power"*
Full Power	**Pull Full Power**	To command the setting of Full Power either pilot may call: *"Pull Full Power"* The PF should then set the collective to the maximum allowable limit to obtain the absolute maximum power available for the day, and respond with: *"Roger, Pull Full Power"*
Maximum Continuous Power	**Maximum Continuous Power**	To command the setting of Maximum Continuous Power either pilot may call: *"Set Max Continuous Power"* The PF should then set Maximum Continuous Power as specified in the AFM and respond with: *"Roger, set max continuous power"*

Item	Call	Description
Abnormal Power	**Check Power**	Upon observing an abnormal Power setting the PM should call: 　　*"Check Power"* The PF should respond with: 　　*"Roger, correcting"* and correct the power to within the normal parameters, **or** if the abnormal power is necessary, call: 　　*"Roger intentional"* and continue.
Heading Deviation	**Heading**	Upon observing a Heading Deviation, the PM should call: 　　*"Heading"* The PF should respond with: 　　*"Roger, correcting"* and correct the aircraft heading. If the PF believes that the aircraft heading is correct as indicated on the PF's display, the flight crew shall determine the source of the discrepancy and deal with it appropriately.
Altitude Deviation	**Altitude**	Upon observing an Altitude Deviation the PM should call: 　　*"Altitude"* The PF should respond with: 　　*"Roger, correcting"* and correct the altitude to within the normal parameters **or** if the abnormal altitude is necessary call: 　　*"Roger intentional"* and continue

Item	Call	Description
Approaching an Altitude	**100ft to go**	Prior to reaching a target altitude the PM shall: - confirm the altitude alert and flight guidance settings (if applicable) - should call the current altitude for target altitude with 300-500ft to spare - then state 100ft to go when 100ft away from the target altitude For example *PM: "1200ft for 1500ft"* *PF: "Roger"* *PM: "100ft to go"* The PF shall respond with: *"Roger"* and then level off at the target altitude
Arriving at an Altitude	**Level at**	Upon arriving at a target altitude the PF should call: *"Level at (Altitude)"* The PM will reply: *"Roger"* and if appropriate make any radio calls to ATC that may be required.

Intentional departures from standard handling

From time to time a pilot may intentionally handle an aircraft outside of the envelope that would normally be expected. Company SOP may or may not allow this but an example may be a descent through a cloud gap to remain VMC.

In these circumstances, the PM is within his rights and should challenge the aircraft handling if the PF has not discussed his intentions beforehand. This scenario highlights the importance of communication. The PF should let the PM know his intentions before-hand so that situational awareness is shared and so that interventions can be better handled.

> **Example**
>
> *"I'm going to increase the rate of descent a little so that we remain VMC"* allows the PM to know what is going on, rather than noticing that the PF is lowering the nose and collective with no explanation as to why.

Using the Radio in an MCC Environment

To foster crew coordination and to avoid misidentification and misinformation in dealing with outside agencies (such as ATC), the crew must communicate effectively. To improve the likelihood that information is passed correctly or that a deviation from the desirable is detected, much of the communication that goes on must be standardised in content and phraseology.

Multi-Crew Cooperation *for Helicopter Pilots*

Radio Procedures

For normal operations both VHF radios should be monitored by all flight crew members. During normal operations the PM is to make any radio transmissions. During abnormal operations, in the absence of the PM, when the PM is engaged in other duties, or should the PIC deem it appropriate, the PF will make any required radio transmissions. Which agency is being addressed on each rado shall be made clear to each flight crew member.

> **Example**

If the number 1 VHF was previously used for communication with the Ground Controller and the PM is now using the number 2 VHF to communicate with the Tower, that change shall be brought to the attention of the remaining flight crew members.

PM: "Switching to Comm 2 and talking to Tower"

Call Sign

For any transmission to ATC or other aircraft the flight crew shall use the full company call sign and flight number as applicable. For example:

"Brisbane Centre Helicopter WCF a Bell206 is overhead Gympie at 2500 tracking 270 for Murgon"

When using a flight number or formation designation then:

"Sunshine Coast Tower Ranger Formation a formation of 3 Jet Rangers is ...."

When talking on the Company frequency then:

"Becker Ops, WCF ...."

Aircraft Internal Communication

Any operational communication whether on the intercom or normal voice shall be acknowledged by the recipient. If it is not acknowledged then the other crew member may think that the communication has not been received.

Although it is not possible to specify all appropriate responses, the following two (2) acknowledgements represent the most commonly used:

- "*Roger*" is the most commonly used form of acknowledgement
  For example: Consider the PM advising the PF that the aircraft has descended to within 100ft of the desired IAP MDA. The appropriate response from the PF would be a simple acknowledgement of "*Roger*".
- "*Check*" is more commonly used in airlines as it infers that as well as acknowledging the communication the PF has also cross checked the information and understands what has been said.

At Becker Helicopters both forms of acknowledgement are acceptable and are deemed to mean the same thing.

MCC Standard Procedures

The following items are standard procedures used during MCC operations:

- Handover and Takeover Procedure
- The Lookout Procedure
- The Hot Swap Procedure
- Altimeter QNH Setting Procedure
- Altitude Alert Setting Procedure
- Radio Altimeter Setting Procedure
- Flight Guidance and Navigation Setting Procedure

Handover Takeover Procedure

This is the procedure to follow when either taking over the helicopters controls from the other pilot (PF/PM) or giving them back to the other pilot (PM/PF).

Important:

It is very important that clear communication is given so there is no doubt who is the pilot actually flying and in control of the helicopter at all times and who the pilot in support is.

Additionally, because most sorties at Becker Helicopters are training sorties (even for multi-crew operations) there is another dynamic in the cockpit and that is between the Instructor and Trainee. For this reason, we have included the Instructor and Trainee profiles in the Handover Takeover description for multi-crew operations.

3 steps

At Becker Helicopters we follow the three (3) step handover takeover procedure for two reasons:

- It is the same procedure that will be used in military organisations where a tandem seating configuration is used (for example, when one pilot is behind the other as used in an Apache, Cobra or Tiger)
- It is the same as that used for NVGs when the pilots cannot actually see each other because it is dark.

Hand over control

When the Pilot Flying (PF) wants to hand over control to the PM complete the following steps.

Step	Announcement	Description
1	PF Handing Over	When the Pilot Flying (PF) wishes to hand over control to the Pilot Monitoring (PM) then say: *"Handing Over"* …but at that time still retain control.
2	PM Taking Over	The PM will then place hands and feet on the controls, take up the instrument scan and when ready to assume control of the aircraft will say: *"Taking Over"*
3	FP You have control	The pilot relinquishing control will confirm that the other pilot is ready to take control by feel and by sight and then say: *"You have control"* …and release the controls.

Take over control

When the PM wishes to re-take control, and therefore, is going to initiate the handover, complete the following steps.

Step	Announcement	Description
1	PM Taking over	When the PM wishes to take control, and therefore, is going to initiate the handover, he/she will place their hands and feet on the controls, take up the instrument scan and when ready to assume control of the aircraft will say: *"Taking over"*
2	PF Handing Over	The PF relinquishing control will then confirm that the other pilot is ready to take control by feel and by sight and then say: *"Handing over"*
3	PM (now the new PF) I have control	The pilot taking control then says *"I have control"* …at which point the pilot relinquishing the controls will release the controls

Abbreviated Takeover procedure

The abbreviated takeover procedure applies during a training scenario.

When there is an instructor with a trainee pilot, there may be an urgent requirement for the instructor to initiate the takeover procedure. The handover may be time critical.

For example, consider the need for the instructor to take over the controls at the bottom of an autorotation or during jammed controls when there is an obvious error by the trainee. The instructor may not have time to wait for the trainee to say the words "**handing over**", before saying the words, "**I have control**".

The exact details on the abbreviated takeover procedure can be covered with the trainee in the pre-flight brief if applicable.

If the student hears the words:

"I have control"

…he/she is to release their controls immediately.

Emphasis by the Instructor will help the trainee understand the urgency of the situation.

Senior Pilots be very clear

When two senior pilots are flying together, the handover procedure must be very clear and adhered to. To avoid any conflict or confusion during the handover, a **lead instructor** for the flight must be nominated prior to the flight commencing. At all times, each person must be very clear who is flying the aircraft.

Follow me through

At times the PF may wish to demonstrate a manoeuvre and have the PM remain on the controls in order to get a feel of the magnitude and rate of control movement.

In this case the PF will say:

"I have control, follow me through"

…at which time the PM will remain lightly on the controls to feel what the PF is doing.

CRM

It is important that both the pilot giving the instruction and the pilot receiving the instruction work as a team and have clear communication as to who is actually in control of the aircraft at any stage of the flight.

When in doubt

If any doubt exists, then the pilot that has the doubt is to communicate this immediately with the other pilot, by saying:

"Who has control"

The other pilot will respond with:

"I have control"

or

"You have control"

…as appropriate.

The Lookout Procedure

Arc of responsibility

During a flight all crew members are given arcs of responsibility in order to maintain an effective lookout.

In the Bell 206BIII the following arcs of responsibility are given:

Scanning Arcs

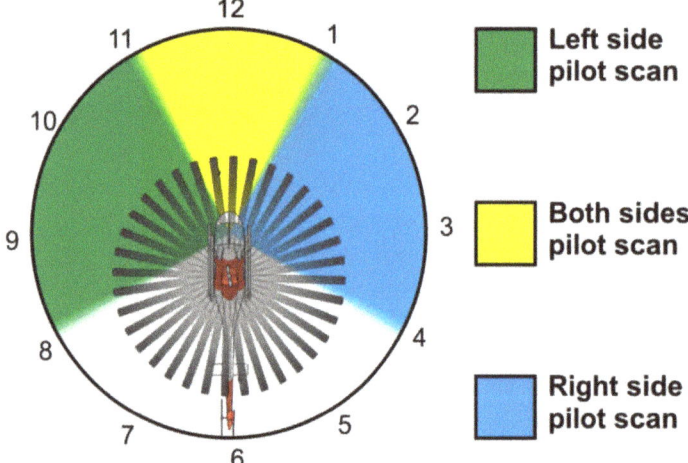

Clearing calls

When making turns the crew members need to move their heads and depending on the arc of responsibility and the next flight manoeuvre, verbally state the clearing calls as follows.

- Clear right
- Clear ahead
- Clear left

Phraseology

When actually doing the clearing checks even though we only say the words Clear right, Clear ahead, Clear left we are in fact looking:

- below,
- same level, and
- above on each of these actions.

Move your head

You move your head in the direction you are looking (for example right) and you then move your eyes to clear below, same level and above.

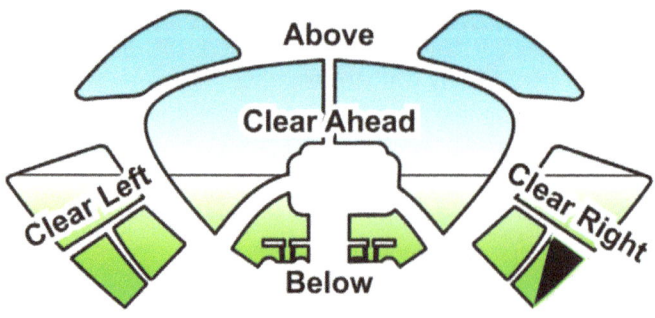

The sequence of words will change depending on the next manoeuvre:

From straight and level flight you wish to:

- do a **left hand turn**, the crew would then:
  - Clear Right, Clear ahead, Clear left – Turning left.
- do a **right hand turn**, the crew would then:
  - Clear left, Clear ahead, Clear right - Turning right.
- **Descend**, the crew would then:
  - Clear right, Clear ahead (with a focus on below) clear left - Descending.

The same procedure applies for any manoeuvre with a particular focus on where you are going after you have cleared the rest of the sky.

The Hot Swap Procedure

The term "Hot Swap" is used to describe one trainee leaving the control seat and being replaced by another while the helicopters engine and blades are still running.

Managing the controls

The approach and departure procedure shall be applied as above but the instructor remaining will be responsible for managing the controls once the trainee leaves the control seat.

Planning

A Hot Swap shall be a pre-planned event with all parties knowing what to do prior to the flight. It can be a dangerous procedure as there is a lot of noise, rotating blades and minimal supervision so the pilot conducting the hot swap shall be well briefed and familiar with opening and closing doors and the approach and departure procedure.

Altimeter QNH Setting Procedure

General

These procedures should be followed for setting the QNH on altimeters in various circumstances.

Receiving an altimeter setting

When receiving an altimeter setting that is either new or unchanged from another ATIS, AWIS or ATC by radio, the applicable flight crew member should write it down and note the time it was taken. If applicable the QNH shall be read back to ATC.

When repeating the QNH either to the crew or to ATC it shall be pre-fixed by the words QNH followed by the actual number:

> **Example**
>
> *"QNH nine nine eight" or "QNH one-zero-one-three"*

Setting the QNH

The QNH will then need to be entered on the subscale of the altimeter(s).

Depending on the helicopter this may include:

- The Primary Altimeter (either analogue or as part of an EFIS display)
- The Standby Altimeter (either analogue or as part of an EFIS display)

The PM will normally be the pilot responsible for tuning into the correct frequency for the ATIS, AWIS or ATC and recording the QNH however both pilots should listen and agree hat the information received is the same as given.

The crew will then set the QNH on the relevant altimeter(s) and then communicate to each other that it has been completed.

> **Example**
>
> ATIS: "Sunshine Coast Terminal Information Bravo. Wind 030/10, RWY 36n use, visibility 10km, cloud FEW at 2500, QNH 1029, Sunshine Coast Terminal Information Bravo"
>
> **PM: will set the QNH on the altimeter closest to him then state "QNH 1029 set left"**
>
> **PF: will set the QNH on the altimeter closest to him then state "QNH 1029 set right"**

Altitude Alert Setting Procedure

The Altitude Alert System shall be used to the extent possible to prevent the pilots inadvertently occupying an altitude other than the altitude desired.

The Altitude Alerting system may be either:

- An analogue device that requires the manual manipulation of tumblers and numbers or
- Part of an EFIS display that is connected to an aural warning system

Setting the Altitude Alert system

When operating as a multi-crew the following procedures should be used for setting the Altitude Alert system:

If the autopilot is engaged then the PF should set the required altitudes in the Altitude Alert System, arm the Flight Guidance System (if applicable) and advise the PM.

> **Example**
>
> **PF: "5500 feet set"**
>
> **PM "Roger"**

If there are two separate Altitude Alert systems, that is one for the PF and one for the PM, then they shall be aligned and both pilots shall notify the other that the same altitude is entered in each system

> **Example**
>
> **PF: "5500 feet set right"**
>
> **PM "5500 feet set left"**

If the auto pilot is *not* engaged and the PF is busy flying the helicopter, then the PM should set the required altitudes in the Altitude Alert System, arm the Flight Guidance System (if applicable) and advise the PF.

For example:

> **Example**
>
> **PM: "5500 feet set"**
>
> **PF "Roger"**

Altitude Confirmation

If ATC give an instruction to maintain or change an altitude then the PM shall respond by reading back the instruction in the normal manner.

After the read back the PM and PF shall go through the same sequence as above for confirming or resetting the Altimeter Alert system.

Radio Altimeter Setting Procedure

General

A Radio Altimeter is installed in helicopters as a supplemental guide to height above the ground for NVFR and IFR but as a mandatory requirement for NVG.

Any flight under the NVFR or IFR shall be at the LSALT or above unless taking off and landing.

Flight under the NVG may be conducted below LSALT therefore the purpose of the procedures described in this section is to reduce the likelihood of inadvertent flight into terrain by setting the RAD ALT and therefore the aural warning system to advise pilots early of rising terrain.

These procedures should be adhered to unless a specific situation dictates a different procedure. In the event that these procedures are deviated from, the aircrew and flight crew shall be fully briefed.

Common RAD ALT setup

The Radio Altimeters (RAD ALTS) have four (4) settings

1. A *variable* setting allowing a pilot to set a value between 0 and 950 feet AGL that an aural warning will activate
2. A *pre-set* aural warning activated at 100 feet AGL regardless of any variable setting by the pilots
3. A *regrade* function that allows the pilots to turn off the 100 foot aural warning when low flying during DAY VFR operations
4. An *OFF* function that sets the RAD ALT to a standby mode so that it does not display heights above the ground and does not give any aural warnings

Setting the RAD ALT

If the autopilot is engaged then the PF should set the required heights AGL on the RAD ALT and advise the PM.

Example

PF: "RAD ALT 500 feet set"
PM "Roger"

If the auto pilot is *not* engaged and the PF is busy flying the helicopter, then the PM should set the required heights AGL on the RAD ALT and advise the PF.

Example

PM: "RAD ALT 500 feet set"
PF "Roger"

The same sequence would apply if turning the RAD ALT to the REGRADE position or the OFF position.

Example

PM: RAD ALT REGRADE"
PF "Roger"

Standard RAD ALT settings

The following settings will apply when using the RAD ALT:

- DAY VFR set the RAD ALT to 950 feet
- NVFR set the RAD ALT to 500 feet
- IFR use the RAD ALT to notify the MDA as required
- NVG set the RAD ALT to 500 feet or lower as required necessary to act as a terrain warning
- REGRADE may be used when conducting low flying DAY VFR
- OFF may be used at the PICs discretion when operating DAY VFR

Alternative settings may be used at the discretion of the PIC but when there is no operational requirement to set a specific RAD ALT setting the above settings shall be used.

Flight Guidance and Navigation System Setting Procedure

The term "Flight Guidance and Navigation System" refers to the combined EFIS displays making available the HSI, RMI, MFD, wind bar, GPS and autopilot information.

In the Bell206BIII helicopters at Becker Helicopters this consists of:

- The ASPEN PFD and MFD displays
- The Garmin 430 GNSS and
- The HeliSAS autopilot

Where practical, the Flight Guidance and Navigation Systems and Displays for each pilot are to be set up in a similar manner so that the information on one is a reflection of the information of the other.

The purpose of this directive is to:

- Make more apparent any deviation away from the desired course.
- Allow both pilots to maintain a high degree of situational awareness by promoting the same or similar mental model of the helicopters position.
- Allow the PF to hand over to the PM and when doing so, reduces the number of things to do with regards to setting up the alternative flight guidance and navigation system.

This objective is fostered by one or both pilots involving the other in the setting of systems, by advising the other pilot of their system status.

Display variation

Individual pilots can assimilate information in different ways and therefore may have different preferences in how they each set up their navigational displays to best interpret the situation.

For this reason, it is not in the best interests of a properly functioning crew to be overly descriptive in directing how a pilot is to set up the navigation displays at a particular pilots' station.

However, some commonality is useful in that crew members can more readily detect inappropriate selections in their own and other displays if there is some common basic coordination requirement.

The following is provided as guidance:

- Both heading bugs should be set to the same heading.
- Both course bars should be set to the same navigation and track information unless one is required to display other information.
- Both displays should be set to the same NAVAID unless otherwise required.
- At least one bearing pointer should be set to display navigation information for the procedure being flown (if applicable).
- Additional bearing pointers may be set to the individual pilots preference.
- Selecting arc, map, HSI, or other on the display can be determined by each pilot provided that sufficient information is displayed for the procedure being flown.

Discrepancy

When both Flight Guidance Displays are set the same and a significant difference beyond the normal limits of display accuracy is observed, then both displays shall be compared to the primary control and navigation displays.

The HSI can be referenced against the magnetic compass which operates independently of the HSI system.

The navigation on the PFD or MFD can be referenced directly to the GPS.

Altitude and speed may be able to be referenced to analogue instruments if they are installed.

If it can be readily determined which display is in error then, then subject to the Flight Manual, MEL, and other sections of the SOPs, flight may be continued using the remaining display.

If both Flight Guidance Displays are found to be in error then they should be removed from view (selected to standby) and the crew will be forced to remain VMC and use alternate instruments if they are available.

With the autopilot engaged

When the autopilot is engaged, and unless workload dictates otherwise, the PF should make all Flight Guidance selections and appropriately advise the PM of the changes which would normally be duplicated by the PM.

With the autopilot dis-engaged

When the autopilot is *not* engaged and the PF is manually flying the helicopter by manipulating the controls, then the PF can request the PMP to make any Flight Guidance selections. On completion of the PM making the changes the PF shall be notified.

Mike Becker

Appendices

Appendix 1: Example STAR Checklist

BECKER HELICOPTERS   FRM-4111

STAR CHECKLIST

Crew Name	ARN	Date
Task Title		**Job No**

Introduction

		Risk:
S	Stop	5 - Extremely High Risk
T	Think	4 - Very High Risk
A	Assess (ask questions get advice)	3 - High Risk
R	Rate the risk and make decisions	2 - Moderate Risk
		1 - Low Risk

Go / No Go Considerations

Approvals and Permissions	Yes	No
What is the aerial work task? (refer to the AOC and Part D of the Operations Manual for Aerial Work categories) – confirm relevant section of Operations Manual read – Identify the relevant sections.	☐	☐
Does the Company have the required approvals to do the aerial work task? Check the expiry date (AOC and Air Maestro)	☐	☐
Does the Company require special CASA approval or dispensation for the aerial work task? (Additional to the approvals already held by the company, for example, flight over a public gathering or air show display or aerobatic display).	☐	☐
Is the Company required to get permission from a third party such as the land owner, local council, police, emergency services, military or similar?	☐	☐
Does the task require a notification period to the general public (for example sling load operations over a high rise building)	☐	☐
Qualifications	**Yes**	**No**
Are you (the pilot in command) approved for this particular aerial work task (Check the Pilot Approval for Special Operations form in your pilot record or Air Maestro) and do you hold the required qualifications (CPL, sling, mustering, ag, low flying, etc.) and are they current. Pilot Approval for Special Operations shows approval for the operation (see Pilot Record and/or Air Maestro) Crew Member Emergency Proficiency Certificate is current for the aircraft type (if required).	☐	☐
What is the pilot in commands overall experience level? If less than 500 hours, Chief Pilot sign-off required.	☐	☐
What is the pilot in commands experience level on the task/operations? If less than 50 hours, Chief Pilot sign-off required.	☐	☐
Operation Planning, Review and Sign-off	**Yes**	**No**
Review site layout? (Google earth, images, maps). Is the site appropriate / safe to conduct operations?	☐	☐
Is a site visit required? (For example, sling load operations, when there are questions about the operating area) On conducting the site visit, is the site appropriate / operations safe to conduct?	☐	☐
Is Chief Pilot (or delegate) sign-off required.	☐	☐

Amendment 02.00 | 27 March 2018   Page 1

Copyright © Becker Helicopter Services Pty Ltd.

Multi-Crew Cooperation *for Helicopter Pilots*

BECKER HELICOPTERS

FRM-4111

STAR CHECKLIST

Risk Assessment

Operational Checklist	Risk (1 to 5)
Are there any crew involved/required? • Company aircrew [3] or • Client [4]	
What location / terrain is involved? • local [1] • over land (not local) [2] • over jungle or in a remote location [3] • over water, desert, or mountainous terrain [4] • polar [5]	
Does the flight involve a public gathering, regatta or other public event? [5]	
Operating under the following flight rules: • DAY VFR [1], • IFR [2], • NVG [3], • NVFR and/or Low level [4]	
Aircraft suitable/available: • Single [3], • Twin (without single engine performance) [2], • Twin (with single engine performance) [1]	
Assess the route including the weather and fuel stops: • Full overcast, foggy, stormy (close to helicopter VMC) [5] • Weather at the minima for the class of airspace [4] • Weather minima plus 500 ft for cloud [3] • Weather minima plus 1000 ft cloud [2] • CAVOK [1]	
Assess the aircraft's performance for the day: • MAUW • Power Margin considered • CAT 1 (limited power take-off) - [4] to [5] • CAT 2 (normal take-off) - [3] • CAT 3 (towering take-off) - [2] • CAT 4 (vertical capability) - [1]	
More than one aircraft involved? • No [1] • Yes [3]	
Fuel supply: • Fuel supplier [1] • Drums [2] • Jerry cans or other [3]	
Fuel availability, within: • 30 nms [1] • 60 nms [2] • 90 nms [3] • 120 nms [4] • 150 nms [5]	
TOTAL	

Any risk assessment of 5 or a risk assessment total greater than 30 requires Chief Pilot sign-off

Amendment 02.00 | 27 March 2018

Copyright © Becker Helicopter Services Pty Ltd.

Mike Becker

BECKER HELICOPTERS   FRM-4111

STAR CHECKLIST

Planning Checklist

Operational Checklist	Yes	No
How many passengers: • Essential personnel only	☐	☐
Is there ground support personnel required/available? (e.g. crowd control, loaders, re-fuellers, etc.)	☐	☐
Safety and emergency equipment: • Water, survival equipment, ELTs • Safety Harness (confirm approval for operations below 1000ft) • For over water operations including life jackets, rafts. • Who needs any training or briefing for the use of this equipment	☐	☐
Ground support equipment required/available? (e.g. re-fuelling equipment, ground markers, ground lighting, fences, etc.) _____ _____	☐	☐
Ancillary equipment required (for example sling, incendiaries, NVGs) _____ _____ _____	☐	☐
Fatigue factors reviewed (see Appendix H6) Detail the fatigue risks and the mitigating strategies to be utilised during this operation: _____ _____ _____ _____ _____	☐	☐
List the identified operational and safety risks and appropriate mitigating strategies: _____ _____ _____ _____ _____	☐	☐
Completed a C of G calculation	☐	☐
Safety brief for all stake holders (e.g. co-pilot, aircrewman, passengers, ground support, client)	☐	☐
Passenger Manifest / cargo manifest	☐	☐
Crew fatigue checks - FAID, Stop Time, Personal Well-Being Rating for all crew checked and noted	☐	☐
Who is holding SAR or a flight note (for flights over water, advise AirServices)	☐	☐

Task Signoff

I certify that I have completed this task assessment and confirm that I have reviewed the operation and planning of the task, and considered and planned for the mitigation of the associated risks, reviewed the planned the operation.

Crew Name and ARN	Signature

Chief Pilot Sign off

Amendment 02.00 | 27 March 2018   Page 3

Copyright © Becker Helicopter Services Pty Ltd.

Multi-Crew Cooperation *for Helicopter Pilots*

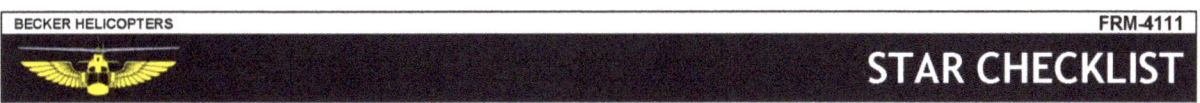

Fatigue Factors: Meaning and mitigating strategies

No	Mitigating Strategies
1	**Cockpit workload** • Multi-crew operations to reduce workload - even an inexperienced pilot in the other seat can help with radio calls, scanning, situational awareness. • Minimum experience level suitable to the operational conditions (been to the airport before) • ICUS / mentoring to build experience with environmental conditions. • Pre-flight planning conducted with pilot experienced with the op conditions • Unfamiliar / non standard operations to be reviewed and signed off by Chief Pilot • Good cockpit organisation, consistent crew procedures and standards, can assist in reducing cockpit workload.
2	**Pilot experience** • If limited experience pilot, arrange for ICUS / mentoring in operations to build up experience. • Set minimum experience levels to jobs / aircraft. • Have experienced pilot assist in the pre-flight planning and briefing.
3	**Passengers / clients involved** • Multi-crew operations to reduce workload - even an inexperienced pilot in the other seat can help with radio calls, scanning, situational awareness. • Assist passengers to prepare for the flight, e.g. will it be hot/cold, should they take a drink / toilet stop, how long the flight will take. • Multi-crew operations when possible / appropriate • Allow adequate time for ground briefing of passengers • Give clear briefings on when and how they can talk to the pilot / crew • Carry out all appropriate weighing, weight and balance calculations, and ensure aircraft is not overloaded. • Remember a happy passenger makes for a much less stressful flight.
4	**Environment** • Minimum experience with the relevant environment (e.g. mountain experience) • ICUS / mentoring to build experience with environmental conditions. • Pre-flight planning conducted with pilot experienced with the op conditions • Dress appropriately for the environment, including variations in the environment (easy to put on or take off clothing layers). • If it is going to be hot, make sure you take plenty of water (and advise the crew and any passengers to take water), • Discuss and agree in pre-flight to the weather minimums and contingency plans • Operate within the agreed weather minimums • Take appropriate supplies to the environmental conditions (e.g. eye drops for dusty operations). • Review aircraft manual and performance limits in relation to environmental extremes (hot, cold, humidity, ice). • Consider doors off for non air-conditioned aircraft (when appropriate to the aircraft). • Pilots should ensure they a well hydrated prior to a flight.
5	**Day or night operations** • Plan your operations to minimise night/late night operations where possible (i.e. leave earlier, leave a buffer time prior to last light) • Plan operations to allow adequate recovery time between night and day operations. • Make sure well rested prior to night operations. • If sleeping during the day, set up bedroom to make it as easy as possible to sleep during the day, e.g. block out curtains. Let your friends and family know you will be working nights and sleeping during the day, and ask them not to call you during the day. Turn off the ringer on your mobile phone and home phone.
6	**Opportunity to rest** • Plan operations to allow opportunity to rest, preferably at least of 15 minutes break every 2 hours. • Find / ask about a good place to take a break (cool, seating, facilities available).
7	**Access to facilities** • Prior to conducting a flight ask about food, water and facilities available • When operating in a remote or unknown area, take water, food and backup supplies (toilet paper). • Prior to travelling to a location, ask about and plan suitable sleeping accommodation. (not shared, air conditioned/heated, curtained, quiet, dark, comfortable)
8	**Variety** • Plan ahead - play "mental games" to keep you alert • Plan check points during the flight • Plan an "interesting" flight path (within operational /fuel limits) • Multi-crew if possible, to provide distraction / support.
9	**Ground support** • Prior to operations consider and plan for the need for ground support / type of ground support required • Have appropriately experienced people on the ground in support. • Pre-brief ground support prior to operation. • Plan all fuel stops, call ahead to ensure sufficient fuel and identify is re-fuelling support is available. • If ground support is not available, allow sufficient ground time to rest/recover.
10	**Location / Travel** • Allow sufficient time to travel to / from the job (allowing for potential travel delays). • Allow sufficient recovery time upon arrival, prior to commencing operations. • Allow for time zone difference when planning operation, e.g. if time difference is 3 hours earlier, try to avoid a take-off time of 6am, which would be 3am base time. • If you haven't been to the location before, find out about the area including health (e.g. malaria), environment (heat, humidity, cold), language and cultural (start work early, late, less time driven) differences.

Appendix 2: Improved Aeronautical Decision Making Can Reduce Accidents

Following is an article written by the Safety Foundation of the UK regarding decision making:[27]

FLIGHT SAFETY FOUNDATION
HELICOPTER SAFETY

Vol. 20 No. 2   For Everyone Concerned with the Safety of Flight   March/April 1994

Improved Aeronautical Decision Making Can Reduce Accidents

Poor pilot decision making plays a leading role in causing aircraft accidents. But proper training can reduce pilot judgment errors significantly.

Joel S. Harris
FlightSafety International

Why do qualified, experienced, professional and mature helicopter pilots continue to have accidents related to poor judgment and bad decision making? "Decision making" refers to the mental process we all use in determining a particular course of action. When used by pilots in conjunction with their flying activities, this process is know as aeronautical decision making (ADM).[1]

The relationship of accidents to pilot ADM and judgment can be summarized as follows:

- Pilot error continues to be a leading cause of aircraft accidents;

- Three U.S. National Transportation Safety Board (NTSB) studies found pilot error the probable cause in as many as 68 percent of rotorcraft accidents;

- Studies of both fixed- and rotary-wing accidents indicate that poor or improper pilot decision making is a leading contributor to pilot-error accidents;

- Six U.S. government-sponsored evaluations of ADM training programs demonstrated that training can reduce pilot judgment errors by as much as 46 percent; and,

- Three operational evaluations of crew resource management (CRM) and ADM training programs specifically for helicopter pilots demonstrated a reduction in human-error accident rates by as much as 54 percent.

Decisional Errors Play a Major Role in Accidents Caused by Pilot Error

A pilot's judgment and decision-making abilities were thought to be largely a by-product of the quality and quantity of flying experience. Nevertheless, beginning in the 1970s, cockpit voice and data recorders and improved accident investigation techniques began to reveal the role played by CRM and ADM in accidents. As a result, in that same decade the U.S. Federal Aviation Administration (FAA) initiated a methodology study of teaching judgment to general aviation pilots.

In an FAA-sponsored study by Jensen and Benel,[2] U.S. general aviation accidents occurring from 1970 to 1974 were analyzed using the NTSB's computerized data base. Air crew errors were divided into three major categories: procedural, perceptualmotor and decisional. Examples of procedural errors included failure to lower the landing gear or overlooking checklist items. Perceptualmotor errors included overshooting a glideslope or stalling an airplane. Decisional errors included failing to delegate tasks in an emergency situation or continuing flight into adverse

---

[27] Harris, Joel S., (1994), FlightSafety Internationl, https://flightsafety.org/hs/hs_mar-apr94.pdf

weather. Jensen and Benel's analysis of fatal accidents involving pilot error indicated that 264 were procedural, 2,496 were perceptualmotor and 2,940 were decisional. In a paper presented in 1991, Alan Diehl analyzed U.S. airline and scheduled air taxi accidents occurring during 1987, 1988 and 1989, using the Jensen and Benel taxonomy. The data indicated that 24 of 28 major accidents involved air crew error.[3] In the 24 accidents involving air crew error, there were 16 procedural, 21 perceptualmotor and 48 decisional errors made. The relative percentages of these errors and the errors in Jensen and Benel's study are depicted in Figure 1.

Although these studies did not address helicopters in particular, an engineering study in 1985 and 1986 of worldwide accidents of Bell civil helicopter models found that poor judgment was the common factor in all human-error accidents.[4]

In two NTSB studies covering the period 1976 to 1981, the pilot was cited as a cause or factor in more than 64 percent of rotorcraft accidents.[5] The FAA conducted an in-depth analysis of one of these studies (the NTSB's *Special Study – Review of Rotorcraft Accidents 1977-1979)*, which cited 890 rotorcraft accidents. It found that decision/judgment errors accounted for 41 percent of the pilot-error accidents (Figure 2, page 3).

The NTSB, in its 1987 study on emergency medical service (EMS) helicopter operations, found that in the 59 EMS helicopter accidents studied, 68 percent involved pilot factors or poor judgment as a part of the probable cause.[6] As a result, the NTSB in that same study recommended that the FAA require ADM training to be incorporated into EMS initial and recurrent training for pilots. In 1991, in an accident summary report issued as a result of a midair collision involving a Piper PA-60 twin-engine fixed-wing aircraft and a Bell 412 helicopter, the NTSB recommended that ADM training be implemented among all categories of pilots in the civil aviation community.[7]

Another definition of ADM is "the ability to search for and establish the relevance of all available information, evaluate alternative courses of action, and the motivation to choose and execute the course of action which assures safety within the timeframe permitted by the situation."[8]

There have been six U.S. government-sponsored independent evaluations of the effectiveness of ADM training programs as they apply to low-time general aviation pilots. Alan Diehl described how these evaluations were performed, after subjects received various types of ADM training:

> The basic criteria were errors made during short, seemingly routine, cross-country 'observation flights.' On these flights, specially trained observers surreptitiously placed subjects in a series of specific decision-making situations (e.g., rushing preflight inspections or suggesting steep maneuvers at low altitudes). Observers then unobtrusively recorded the errors on these judgment items. In these rigorous 'double-blind' experiments, the observers were not informed which subjects had received ADM training, while subjects were unaware of the real purpose of the flights beforehand (e.g., subjects might be led to believe they would be evaluating new map designs.)[9]

The evaluations showed that the effectiveness of ADM training varied depending on the type of training received. In the six studies, improvement in the subjects' aeronautical decision making ranged from 8 percent in a voluntary,

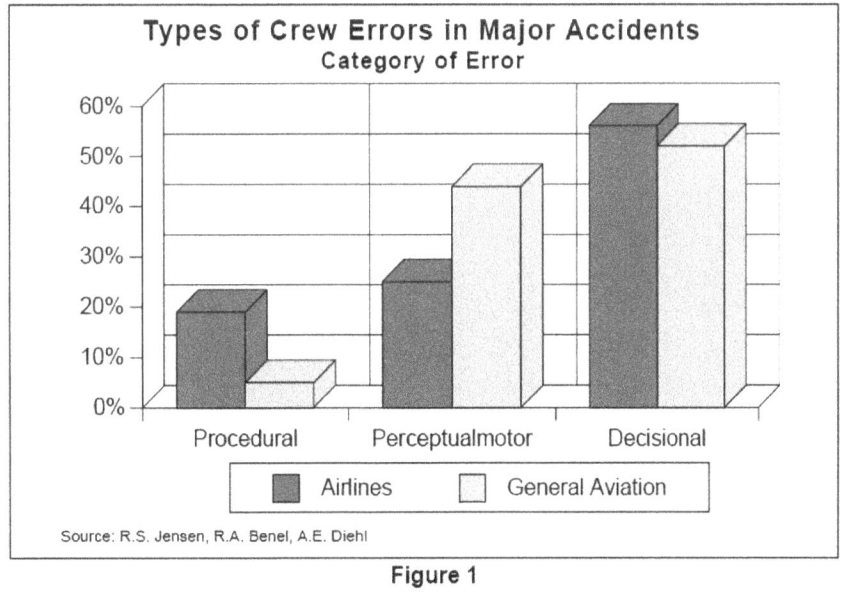

Figure 1

minimally structured training program to 46 percent in a well-structured, comprehensive, ground school environment that included simulator training.

These six studies provided strong statistical evidence that ADM training can improve pilot decision making and judgment in low-time pilots. The real test of the effectiveness of ADM training is in its contribution to the reduction of accidents.

Helicopter Accidents Reduced by ADM Training

Categorical distinctions between CRM and ADM are disappearing because comprehensive versions of these programs have common functional components. Comprehensive CRM training programs almost always include elements of decision making.

The U.S. Navy began comprehensive, formal CRM training at all Navy and Marine Corps helicopter training units in 1987. The air crew error rate for mishaps was 7.01 when the training program began. By 1990, the rate had been reduced to 5.05, a 28 percent improvement.[9]

Based on the findings of the engineering study that found poor judgment to be the common factor in Bell helicopter human-error accidents, Bell launched an aggressive judgment-training program for helicopter pilots in 1987.[10] By 1990, the human-error accident rates for the Bell Model 206 had fallen from 3.9 per 100,000 flight hours to 2.49 per 100,000 flight hours, a reduction of 36.2 percent. Petroleum Helicopter Inc. (PHI), the largest commercial helicopter operator in the United States, began ADM training in mid-1986. Chief Pilot Vernon Albert reported in *Rotor & Wing* magazine that:

> From 1980 through 1986, we had an accident rate of about 2.3 accidents per 100,000 flight hours. In mid-1986, we started ADM training, and the rate in 1987 was 1.86 and then dropped to 1.05 in 1988. The only thing we changed in our training syllabus was adding ADM and cockpit resources management.[11]

These figures represented a reduction in overall accidents of 54 percent after PHI began ADM training for its helicopter pilots.

Vernon Albert said in a recent interview that PHI continues to successfully incorporate CRM and ADM training in its pilot training courses.

"PHI is flying over 200,000 rotorcraft hours annually and the accident rate has continued to diminish and is now less than 1.0 per 100,000 flight hours," Albert said.[12]

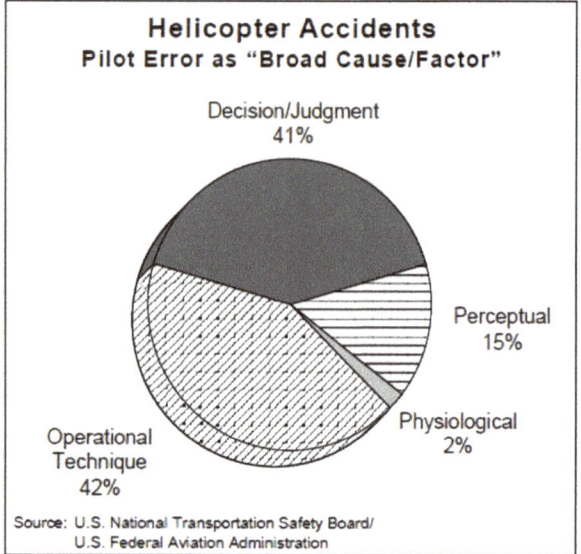

Figure 2

A comparison of the reduction in helicopter accidents after implementation of ADM and CRM training in these three instances is shown in Figure 3 (page 4).

The FAA and Transport Canada have developed versions of ADM training manuals for helicopter pilots. These manuals are widely used by major rotorcraft organizations. The FAA also produced a published series that includes four ADM training publications:

- *Aeronautical Decision Making for Helicopter Pilots;*

- *Aeronautical Decision Making for EMS Helicopter Pilots — Learning from Past Mistakes;*

- *Aeronautical Decision Making for EMS Helicopter Pilots — Situational Awareness Exercises;* and,

- *Risk Management for Air Ambulance Operators.*

FlightSafety International (FSI) introduced ADM into its curriculum in 1989. Initially, decision making was taught by a classroom presentation supplemented by the use of an interactive computer. In 1992, the company's helicopter instructor staff at the West Palm Beach Sikorsky Learning Center was trained in development and implementation of decision-making scenarios for use in the simulator. Each scenario is called a "SPOT" (Special Purpose Operational Training) and consists of a short operational simulator flight that is designed to provide pilots with opportunities to practice decision-making skills in a real-time environment. One of the interesting sides to the training is that pilots are not graded or critiqued on the decisions they reach but only on the process by which they reach them. The pilots determine if the decisions that they made were the best possible given all of the facts. During the post-flight debriefing, which may be augmented by reviewing videotaped segments of the flight, the decision-making process is carefully examined. Did the pilot follow the fundamental steps required in reaching a good decision? Some experienced instructors feel that aggressive decision making may be part of the pilot personality profile. FSI CRM training specialist Ken Westerlund said:

> Helicopter pilots, and perhaps all pilots, have a tendency to make decisions quickly, sometimes without gathering all available information. This type of decision making may be a result of a number of factors including self-confidence, faith in one's ability and training. Most of our customers are former military pilots.[13] Military pilot training historically has heavily stressed immediate action by memory in emergencies. In modern twin-turbine helicopters, few emergencies actually require the pilot to take immediate action, and when they do an accelerated memory response is appropriate. In most cases, however, time is available for the pilot to make use of the full decision-making model.

When available time is assessed and used properly, there is evidence that success rates increase. In an FSI study of flight crews using a Bell 222 visual/motion simulator, pilots were given a catastrophic tail-rotor failure shortly after takeoff. Those instructed to land immediately upon encountering the failure crashed in more than 80 percent of the cases. However, pilots instructed to climb to a safe altitude and stabilize there until they felt more prepared to land crashed less than 20 percent of the time.[14]

An established aeronautical decision-making process such as the one described below helps organize thoughts and addresses the situation or problem in an objective manner.

The decision-making process begins after a need is recognized. An example might be a the illumination of a caution light or an engine gauge out of limits.

After the need is recognized, the first step in the decision-making process is to clearly identify the problem. This is a step that flight crews often overlook. After a caution light illuminates, for example, crew members may "jump to conclusions" concerning the nature of the problem, instead of taking the time to get the "big picture." Is the caution light the only indication of a malfunction, or is it a symptom of a larger problem? Can the light be confirmed by other indications? If operating in a multi-crew cockpit, verbal agreement as to the identity of the problem and the conditions that need to change should be reached. Identifying the problem also allows the crew to assess the approximate time available to complete the decision-making process. If the problem requires an immediate or a very rapid response, an "accelerated response" may be necessary.

It is important to access all available sources of information. Time may or may not be a limiting factor. Some malfunctions, for example, pose no immediate threat to the crew, such as a landing gear stuck in the retracted position. In such cases, the crew should recognize that time to complete the decision-making process may only be limited by the aircraft fuel supply.

Some of the resources available to the crew for fact collection may include other crew members, aircraft gauges and sensations, air traffic control (ATC), other aircraft, flight manuals, checklists, other documentation and ground-based support. Ultimately, the final decision will be no better than the information collected during this crucial phase of the process.

Another often overlooked area in the decision-making process is identifying as many alternative courses of action as possible. When identifying alternatives, crews need to consider beyond the obvious choices. Careful identification of all alternative courses of action greatly enhances the decision-making process and helps assure the best possible outcome.

Careful and accurate assessment of the influence of each alternative must now be made. The pros and cons of each alternative are weighed and evaluated.

Make a decision as a result of the process. If the pilot has collected as many facts and identified as many alternatives

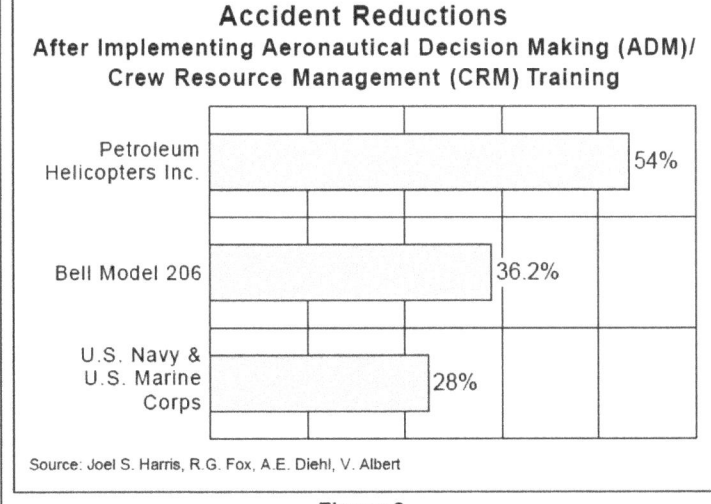

Accident Reductions
After Implementing Aeronautical Decision Making (ADM)/
Crew Resource Management (CRM) Training

- Petroleum Helicopters Inc.: 54%
- Bell Model 206: 36.2%
- U.S. Navy & U.S. Marine Corps: 28%

Source: Joel S. Harris, R.G. Fox, A.E. Diehl, V. Albert

Figure 3

as time allows, and thoughtfully weighed the influence of each alternative, choosing a good response should not be difficult.

Take timely action to implement the chosen response. Or, if at this point additional time is available, the crew may decide to consider a deliberate delay in implementing the response, choosing instead to collect more facts or to identify additional alternatives or to reassess the influence of various alternative responses.

Monitor the effect of the response chosen. Keep an open mind. There is often a tendency to stick with a decision even though there is new information that suggests the need to reevaluate. Do not take the position, "It's my decision and I'm going to stick with it, no matter what." As new information becomes available, renew the decision-making process and repeat it until the problem has been successfully resolved.

Good judgment is the capacity to make responsible choices. Judgment affects decision making. Some of the factors that affect judgment are experience, training, workload, time pressure, stress, fatigue, situational awareness and attitude. Some constructive attitudes that enhance a pilot judgment include:

- A positive "can-do" spirit;
- Open-mindedness;
- Willingness to listen;
- Optimism;
- Cooperation; and,
- Teamwork.

Disruptive attitudes interfere with effective crew performance. The FAA has identified the following hazardous attitudes:[1]

- Anti-authority: "Don't tell me!"
- Impulsivity: "Do something — quickly!"
- Invulnerability: "It won't happen to me."
- Machismo: "I can do it."
- Resignation: "What's the use?"

In certain situations, time is a severe limitation to the decision-making process. When time is short, an accelerated response may be necessary. Standardization of procedures and training prepares pilots for accelerated responses. The advantage of standardized procedures such as checklists, flight manuals and standard operating procedures (SOPs) is that many of the critical decision functions will have been accomplished previously under ideal conditions. Some SOPs recognize that time is critical. In such a case, facts will have already been collected, alternatives identified, influence of alternatives weighed and the best response selected. In critical or emergency situations, these predetermined procedures reduce time and workload, allowing the crews to safely get from need recognition to response selection.

Decision making is the process of recognizing the need to make a decision, identifying the problem, collecting facts, identifying alternatives, weighing their influence and selecting and implementing a response.

Judgment and decision making are related, and many factors can and do affect judgment. Pilots must guard against hazardous attitudes that degrade judgment and decision-making skills.

Using the decision-making process gives the pilot an organized method of solving problems and implementing decisions. ♦

References

1. Adams, R.J. and Thompson, J.L. *Aeronautical Decision Making for Helicopter Pilots*, U.S. Department of Transportation (DOT)/U.S. Federal Aviation Administration (FAA) Report No. DOT/FAA/PM-86/45. February 1987.

2. Jensen, R.S. and Benel, R.A. *Judgment Evaluation and Instruction in Civil Pilot Training*, U.S. Department of Transportation (DOT)/U.S. Federal Aviation Administration (FAA) Report No. DOT/FAA/RD-78-24. 1977.

3. Diehl, A.E. "The Effectiveness of Training Programs in Preventing Aircrew Error." In *Proceedings of the Sixth International Symposium of Aviation Psychology*. Columbus, Ohio, United States: Ohio State University, 1991. Cited in Diehl, A.E. "Does Cockpit Management Training Reduce Aircrew Error?" Paper presented at the 22nd International Seminar of the International Society of Air Safety Investigators. Canberra, Australia, November 1991.

4. Fox, R.G. "Helicopter Accident Trends." Paper presented at American Helicopter Society/Helicopter Association International/U.S. Federal Aviation Administration seminar "Vertical Flight Training Needs and Solutions." September 1987. Cited in Fox, R.G. "Measuring Risk in Single and Twin Engine Helicopters." In *Proceedings of Aeronautical Decision*

Making Workshop. Jupiter, Florida, United States: Advanced Aviation Concepts, 1992.

5. U.S. National Transportation Safety Board, *Annual Review of Aircraft Accident Data — U.S. General Aviation 1981 and Special Study — Review of Rotorcraft Accidents 1977-1979.* Cited in Adams, R.J. and Thompson, J.L. *Aeronautical Decision Making for Helicopter Pilots,* U.S. Department of Transportation (DOT)/U.S. Federal Aviation Administration (FAA) Report No. DOT/FAA/PM-86/45. February 1987.

6. National Transportation Research Board. *Safety Study — Commercial Emergency Medical Service Helicopter Operations.* January 1988.

7. U.S. National Transportation Safety Board (NTSB). *Aircraft Accident Summary Report, Midair Collision Involving Lycoming Air Service PA-60 and Sun Oil Bell 4-12,* NTSB Report No. AAR-91-01. 1991.

8. *Judgment Evaluation and Instruction in Civil Pilot Training,* Report No. FAA-RD78-24. A special report prepared at the request of the U.S. Federal Aviation Administration (FAA). December 1978.

9. Diehl, A.E. "Does Cockpit Management Training Reduce Aircrew Error?" Paper presented at the 22nd International Seminar of the International Society of Air Safety Investigators. Canberra, Australia, November 1991.

10. Fox, R.G. "Measuring Risk in Single and Twin Engine Helicopters." In *Proceedings of Aeronautical Decision Making Workshop.* Jupiter, Florida, United States: Advanced Aviation Concepts, 1992.

11. Albert, V. Interviewed in *Rotor & Wing International.* Volume 23 (November 1989). Cited in Diehl, A.E. "Does Cockpit Management Training Reduce Aircrew Error?" Paper presented at the 22nd International Seminar of the International Society of Air Safety Investigators. Canberra, Australia, November 1991.

12. Albert, V. Telephone interview by Harris, J.S. West Palm Beach, Florida, United States. 22 March 1994.

13. Adams, R. "Simulator Usage Questionnaire Composite Results." Jupiter, Florida, United States: Advanced Aviation Concepts, 1991.

14. Schwartz, D. "Cockpit Management — The Safety Window." In *30 Years — And Still Training for Safety, Proceedings of the 30th Annual Corporate Aviation Safety Seminar.* Arlington, Virginia, United States: Flight Safety Foundation, 1985.

About the Author

Joel S. Harris holds an airline transport pilot certificate and a flight instructor certificate with ratings in both helicopters and airplanes. He is an instructor, supervisor and courseware developer at FlightSafety International's West Palm Beach Learning Center in Florida, U.S. He has given more than 10,000 hours of flight, simulator and ground school training to professional helicopter pilots. Harris is the author of numerous articles about helicopter flight.

HELICOPTER SAFETY
Copyright © 1994 FLIGHT SAFETY FOUNDATION INC. ISSN 1042-2048

Suggestions and opinions expressed in FSF publications belong to the author(s) and are not necessarily endorsed by Flight Safety Foundation. Content is not intended to take the place of information in company policy handbooks and equipment manuals, or to supersede government regulations.

Staff: Roger Rozelle, director of publications; Girard Steichen, assistant director of publications; Kate Achelpohl, editorial assistant; and Dwyane D. Feaster, production consultant.

Subscriptions: US$60 (United States-Canada-Mexico), US$65 Air Mail (all other countries), six issues yearly. • Include old and new addresses when requesting address change. • Flight Safety Foundation, 2200 Wilson Boulevard, Suite 500, Arlington, VA 22201-3306 U.S. • telephone: (703) 522-8300 • telex: 901176 FSF INC AGTN • fax: (703) 525-6047.

We Encourage Reprints
Articles in this publication may be reprinted in whole or in part, but credit must be given to Flight Safety Foundation, *Helicopter Safety,* the specific article and the author. Please send two copies of reprinted material to the director of publications.

What's Your Input?
In keeping with FSF's independent and nonpartisan mission to disseminate objective safety information, Foundation publications solicit credible contributions that foster thought-provoking discussion of aviation safety issues. If you have an article proposal, a completed manuscript or a technical paper that may be appropriate for *Helicopter Safety,* please contact the director of publications. Reasonable care will be taken in handling a manuscript, but Flight Safety Foundation assumes no responsibility for material submitted. The publications staff reserves the right to edit all published submissions. Payment is made to author upon publication. Contact the Publications Department for more information.

Appendix 3: Air Ambulance Strikes Terrain After Takeoff in Fog

An article from the Flight Safety Foundation.[28]

Vol. 29 No. 2   *For Everyone Concerned With the Safety of Flight*   **March–April 2003**

Air Ambulance Strikes Terrain After Takeoff in Fog

Visibility was less than 0.25 statute mile (0.40 kilometer) when the crew of the Sikorsky S-76A began the night repositioning flight. Less than two minutes after takeoff, the helicopter struck a tree-covered hillside.

FSF Editorial Staff

At 2208 local time June 14, 1999, a Sikorsky S-76A helicopter being operated by Petroleum Helicopters Inc. (PHI) as an air ambulance for the University of Kentucky Medical Center (37KY) at Lexington, Kentucky, U.S., collided with terrain in instrument meteorological conditions (IMC) during departure from Jackson, Kentucky. The helicopter was destroyed, and all four people in the helicopter — two pilots and two medical crewmembers — were killed.

The U.S. National Transportation Safety Board (NTSB) said, in its final report, that the probable cause of the accident was "the failure of the PIC [pilot-in-command] to adequately supervise the SIC [second-in-command] and maintain a positive climb." The report said that factors in the accident were fog and dark-night conditions.

The 49-year-old PIC held a commercial pilot certificate with rotorcraft-helicopter and instrument-helicopter ratings; he had a second-class medical certificate with a requirement that he have corrective lenses for near vision in his possession. He learned to fly helicopters in the U.S. Army and was hired in 1984 by PHI. He had accumulated 6,859 flight hours, including 2,319 flight hours in S-76As. His instrument flight experience totaled 382 flight hours, including 111 hours in simulators and 39 flight hours in actual IMC.

The report said that his initial checkout in an S-76A was as an SIC in February 1990. During a March 1996 six-month recurrent instrument flight check, one item — "stabilized approach concept" — initially was recorded as unsatisfactory and later recorded as satisfactory. The check airman's written remarks said that the pilot failed to call for a missed approach "with the airspeed 25 knots slow."

In September 1991, the pilot was upgraded to PIC. In March 1997, he failed a six-month recurrent instrument flight check. The report said that the PIC "was rated unsatisfactory in the following areas: use of checklists, emergency procedures, flight planning, ILS [instrument landing system] approaches, VOR [very-high-frequency omnidirectional radio] approaches and missed approach." The check airman made a number of written remarks, including, in reference to flight planning, that "he did not understand the operations manual with regard to IFR [instrument flight rules] takeoff minimums." The next day, the PIC repeated the check ride and passed all items. He also passed check rides in September 1997 and April 1998.

He received training in the Bell 412 in 1998 and passed an SIC check ride. The report said that training records "noted several areas of deficiency found during the training" and included the following remarks: "unstabilized ILS at middle marker" and "before takeoff IFR, nav [navigation] and com [communication] radios — airman was confused about [a functional] check and what radios were displayed where." The pilot re-qualified in

---

[28] FSF Editorial Staff (2003), https://flightsafety.org/hs/hs_mar-apr03.pdf

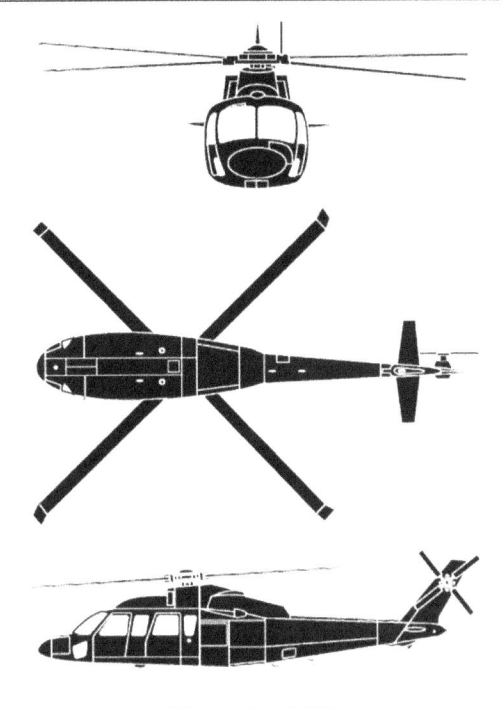

Sikorsky S-76

The Sikorsky S-76 first flew in 1977. The S-76A is configured to accommodate 12 passengers and two pilots. It has a maximum takeoff weight of 10,300 pounds (4,672 kilograms), a maximum cruising speed of 145 knots and a service ceiling of 15,000 feet. The S-76A has a maximum range of 404 nautical miles (748 kilometers) with 12 passengers, standard fuel and 30-minute reserves. The S-76A is powered by two Allison 250-C30 turboshaft engines, each rated at 650 shaft horsepower (485 kilowatts).♦

Source: *Jane's All the World's Aircraft*

the S-76A as PIC in September 1998 and passed a six-month recurrent instrument flight check in February 1999.

The 46-year-old SIC held a commercial pilot certificate with ratings for airplane, single-engine land; airplane multi-engine land; and rotorcraft-helicopter. He also held instrument ratings for airplanes and helicopters and a mechanic certificate with an airframe rating and a powerplant rating. He was issued a first-class medical certificate in August 1998. He had accumulated 7,739 flight hours, including 6,574 flight hours in helicopters. His instrument flight experience totaled 181 flight hours, including 92 flight hours in actual IMC.

Company records showed that he was hired as a maintenance technician in 1976 and subsequently participated in a company program to become a pilot. He began flying single-engine helicopters in 1982. His initial checkout in the S-76A occurred in May 1997, and he passed two subsequent six-month recurrent instrument flight checks. In May 1998, he failed an oral exam required to become an S-76A PIC; the flight check was not conducted.

Training records said that the SIC was "weak in several areas related to instrument procedures and flight planning." Another oral examination was administered in June 1998, and he requalified as an S-76A SIC. He subsequently passed two six-month recurrent instrument flight checks.

In post-accident interviews, other pilots from the operator's Lexington base said that the two pilots often flew together.

"Both pilots were reported to have demonstrated varying degrees of assertiveness in the cockpit," the report said. "No negative comments were generated for either pilot. However, one pilot did report that the SIC told him he felt uncomfortable flying with the PIC under IFR conditions. No specifics were given for the reported statement of the SIC."

The S-76A is type-certificated for two pilots when operated under IFR. The accident helicopter was one of two medical helicopters operated by PHI from 37KY. The helicopter was equipped with three sets of attitude indicators and directional indicators. The helicopter also was equipped with dual VOR receivers, distance-measuring equipment (DME) and an IFR-approved global positioning system (GPS) receiver. The helicopter did not have an autopilot. The helicopter was equipped with a cockpit voice recorder (CVR) and continually energized lip microphones at the first pilot's station and second pilot's station.

During the six months before the accident, two attitude indicators and three vertical gyros on the accident helicopter had been replaced. At the time of the accident, PHI operated 24 S-76 helicopters, and company records showed that, during the same six-month period, 40 vertical gyros on 15 helicopters and 11 attitude indicators on seven helicopters had been replaced.

The morning of the accident, the flight crew reported for duty at 1100 hours at 37KY. They were on the fourth day of a seven-day rotation, and their shift was to end 12 hours later, at 2300.

At 1356, the crew began a flight to reposition the helicopter to Julian Carroll Airport (JKL), an uncontrolled airport at the top of a hill at 1,381 feet in Jackson, Kentucky, about 67 nautical miles (124 kilometers) southeast of Lexington. JKL had no published takeoff criteria for Runway 19, which was equipped with medium-intensity runway edge lights. There was a VOR/DME and GPS approach to Runway 1.

The helicopter was landed at JKL at 1426. At JKL, the helicopter was fueled with 35 gallons (132 liters) of Jet-A fuel with an anti-icing fuel additive. The crew had access to a lounge area for rest. The lounge contained a computer with a direct user access terminal system (DUATS), which could be used to check weather and file flight plans. Records from the U.S. Federal Aviation Administration showed that the PIC had used DUATS three times in preparation for their night flight to reposition the helicopter to 37KY.

The first time was at 1912, when he requested an abbreviated weather briefing for the state of Kentucky, including aviation routine weather reports (METARs) and aerodrome forecasts (TAFs) with data for JKL and Blue Grass Airport in Lexington, near 37KY. The second time was at 2005, when he filed an IFR flight plan for a direct flight from JKL to the Lexington VOR but did not request weather data. The third time was at 2121, about 45 minutes before the flight, when he requested an abbreviated weather briefing for the state of Kentucky, including METARs and TAFs. JKL weather at that time included calm winds and visibility of 0.5 statute mile (0.8 kilometer), with the sky obscured, vertical visibility of 100 feet and fog. The temperature and dew point both were 18 degrees Celsius (C; 64 degrees Fahrenheit).

The flight to 37KY was planned to take 30 minutes.

The airport manager at JKL said that he observed the crew in the lounge, planning an IFR flight to Lexington, and that "they had a manual out and were talking about maintaining a 250-feet-a-minute rate of climb to 3,000 feet."

"The airport manager observed the flight crew walk to the helicopter," the report said. "He reported that visibility was reduced by fog, and he could not recognize the pilots but only saw vague shapes as they boarded the helicopter."

At 2154, after boarding the aircraft and starting both engines, the crew checked the JKL automated surface observations system (ASOS). The ASOS information, which was recorded several times by the CVR, said that visibility at JKL was less than 0.25 statute mile (0.40 kilometer) in fog, the sky was overcast with a ceiling of 200 feet, and the temperature and dew point were 18 degrees C.

The CVR did not record any comments by the crew about the visibility being less than 0.25 mile. Although the flight was conducted under U.S. Federal Aviation Regulations Part 91, which does not specify IFR takeoff minimums for Part 91 operators, the chief pilot said that he expected company pilots always to follow the guidance contained in the company *Air Taxi Operations Manual* for Part 135 flights. The manual said that "one-quarter statute mile or touchdown zone RVR [runway visual range] of 1,200 [feet] may be used if either HIRL (high-intensity runway lights), CL (centerline lights), RCLM (runway centerline markings), or adequate visual reference to continuously identify the takeoff surface of the runway and maintain directional control throughout the takeoff run is available."

Subsequent interviews with the pilots at the Lexington base confirmed that they all believed that the IFR section of the *Air Taxi Operations Manual*, including takeoff minimums, applied to flights conducted under Part 91. Several pilots said that this requirement was discussed as a regular part of their recurrent training.

At 2159, the flight crew contacted Indianapolis (Indiana, U.S.) Air Route Traffic Control Center (ARTCC) and requested activation of their flight plan and an IFR clearance. ARTCC asked if the helicopter was in the air, and the crew replied that they were "sitting on the ramp at Julian Carroll" and would be "ready to go in five minutes." ARTCC issued the clearance and told the crew to climb to and maintain 4,000 feet.

The CVR recorded the sounds of the crew conducting a checklist; checking radios, instruments and other equipment; and setting the radar altimeter to 500 feet before beginning to taxi the helicopter to Runway 19.

Soon after 2200, the airport manager heard the PIC say on the UNICOM (a communication radio frequency used to broadcast information at some airports) that the helicopter was taking off on Runway 19.

The PIC said, "We'll be a, uh … south departure, right turn, we, be, uh, west out of the area." The crew then lifted the helicopter to a hover.

A certified weather observer at JKL, who had just completed an hourly observation, observed the takeoff.

"When they rolled onto the runway, I walked out to watch them take off," he said. "At the runway/taxiway intersection, they turned left for Runway 19 and pulled up into a hover about 20 feet above the runway. They then proceeded down Runway 19. I lost [sight of] them in the fog about half way between the taxi/runway intersection and the end of the runway. As a certified weather observer, I concur with the ASOS visibility of (less than) one-quarter mile. I estimate that the visibility was about one-eighth of a [statute] mile [0.2 kilometer] or slightly more."

At 2206:18, the CVR recorded the SIC on the interphone as he said, "I'm gonna lift to a hover, and we'll get 60 knots before we get solid in it, I guess. Try to keep it with the lights down here." The PIC acknowledged the SIC's statement.

At 2206:28, the SIC said on interphone, "Here we go." This was followed by a sound similar to transient main-rotor droop (the temporary decrease in main-rotor speed after an application of power).

At 2206:51, the PIC said, "Airspeed's alive, positive rate of climb. … You're at 30 (knots) … heading one nine zero. … I'm gonna kill the landing (lights)." The SIC acknowledged the statement.

At 2207:22, the PIC said, "You're at 80 … wanna hold 80, or V_{broc} (velocity best rate of climb)." [In an S-76A, V_{broc} is 74 knots at sea level.]

At 2207:32, the PIC said, "Indy [Indianapolis] Center, Sikorsky two seven four three echo. We're, ah, passing one thousand six hundred for four thousand."

At 2207:51, the PIC said on the interphone, "Go ahead and stay on your heading."

At 2208:03, the PIC said, "OK, you're in a right-hand turn and descending."

The SIC replied at 2208:05 "OK, I think my gyro just quit." There was no acknowledgement from the PIC.

At 2208:10, the SIC asked, "You have the controls?"

The PIC did not answer the question but said, "You're in a left-hand turn and descending … turn … turn back and level, level us off." There was no acknowledgement from the SIC.

At 2208:16, the CVR recorded an increase in ambient noise.

At 2208:18, the PIC said, "right-hand turn … right-hand turn." There was no acknowledgement from the SIC.

At 2208:24, the CVR recorded the initial sound of the impact and then stopped functioning.

The aircraft struck terrain 116 seconds after departure from JKL.

ARTCC radar data showed that the helicopter initially was flown to 1,600 feet. Then, while in a left turn, the helicopter began to descend. The final radar contact at 2208:14 showed the helicopter at 1,300 feet.

A witness who lived near the accident site said that he heard the helicopter while he was inside his home and that he went outside and "heard a pop, saw a bright flash, then — silence." He said that about 30 seconds to 45 seconds later, he "saw and heard a large explosion" at the accident site and called law enforcement authorities.

The burned wreckage was found on a tree-covered slope approximately 1,000 feet above mean sea level, or 381 feet below the elevation of the departure airport, which was about two nautical miles (3.7 kilometers) northwest of the accident site.

After the accident, PHI said in a letter to NTSB that the company, which already provided initial training and recurrent training in crew resource management (CRM), had "enhanced our crew concept procedures" to include mandatory use of CRM principles and expansion of the stabilized-approach concept to other phases of flight. The chief pilot said that the company had begun using line-oriented simulations (LOS) during simulator training to include CRM debriefings that were designed to challenge the CRM abilities of the flight crew. If the LOS sessions reveal "serious shortcomings in procedure or CRM," crewmembers receive additional training, he said.♦

[FSF editorial note: This article, except where specifically noted, is based on the U.S. National Transportation Safety Board final report on accident no. NYC99FA140. The report comprises 218 pages and includes photographs, a map and figures.]

Want more information about Flight Safety Foundation?

Contact Ann Hill, director, membership and development,
by e-mail: hill@flightsafety.org or by telephone: +1 (703) 739-6700, ext. 105.

Visit our Internet site at <www.flightsafety.org>.

We Encourage Reprints

Articles in this publication, in the interest of aviation safety, may be reprinted, in whole or in part, but may not be offered for sale, used commercially or distributed electronically on the Internet or on any other electronic media without the express written permission of Flight Safety Foundation's director of publications. All uses must credit Flight Safety Foundation, *Helicopter Safety*, the specific article(s) and the author(s). Please send two copies of the reprinted material to the director of publications. These restrictions apply to all Flight Safety Foundation publications. Reprints must be ordered from the Foundation.

What's Your Input?

In keeping with FSF's independent and nonpartisan mission to disseminate objective safety information, Foundation publications solicit credible contributions that foster thought-provoking discussion of aviation safety issues. If you have an article proposal, a completed manuscript or a technical paper that may be appropriate for *Helicopter Safety*, please contact the director of publications. Reasonable care will be taken in handling a manuscript, but Flight Safety Foundation assumes no responsibility for material submitted. The publications staff reserves the right to edit all published submissions. The Foundation buys all rights to manuscripts and payment is made to authors upon publication. Contact the Publications Department for more information.

Helicopter Safety
Copyright © 2003 by Flight Safety Foundation Inc. All rights reserved. ISSN 1042-2048

Suggestions and opinions expressed in FSF publications belong to the author(s) and are not necessarily endorsed by
Flight Safety Foundation. Content is not intended to take the place of information in company policy handbooks
and equipment manuals, or to supersede government regulations.

Staff: Roger Rozelle, director of publications; Mark Lacagnina, senior editor; Wayne Rosenkrans, senior editor; Linda Werfelman, senior editor;
Rick Darby, associate editor; Joel S. Harris, editorial consultant; Karen K. Ehrlich, web and print production coordinator; Ann L. Mullikin,
production designer; Susan D. Reed, production specialist; and Patricia Setze, librarian, Jerry Lederer Aviation Safety Library

Subscriptions: One year subscription for six issues includes postage and handling: US$240. Include old and new addresses when requesting address change. • Attention: Ahlam Wahdan, membership services coordinator, Flight Safety Foundation, Suite 300, 601 Madison Street, Alexandria, VA 22314 U.S. • Telephone: +1 (703) 739-6700 • Fax: +1 (703) 739-6708

Terms and Abbreviations

Abbreviation	Meaning
ATC	Air Traffic Control
CRM	Crew Resource Management
IFR	Instrument Flight Rules
IMC	Instrument Meteorological Conditions
LSALT	Lowest Safe Altitude
MCC	Multi-Crew Cooperation
NUA	Night Unaided
NVFR	Night Visual Flight Rules
NVG	Night Vision Goggles
PF	Pilot Flying
PIC	Pilot in Command
PM	Pilot Monitoring
SIC	Second in Command
SOP	Standard Operating Procedure
STAR	Stop, Think, Assess, Rate
TEM	Threat Error Management
UAS	Undesired Aircraft State
VFR	Visual Flight Rules

Bibliography

Please find below citations to books, websites, or images referenced during this book's authoring.

- Aviation Risk Management: An Introduction (Booklet Four) by Civil Aviation Authority of New Zealand. www.caa.govt.nz/SMS/sms_booklet_4.pdf
- SMS Guidance Manual by IBAC.
- Guidelines for the Conduct of Risk Analyses by Business Aircraft Operations, IBAC 2003.
- Risk Management Handbook (FAA-H-8083-2).
- Threat and Error Management (TEM) SafeSkies Presentation, Ian Banks, Section Head, Human Factors, CASA, 27 Aug 2011 https://www.casa.gov.au/sites/g/files/net351/f/_assets/main/lib100030/banks-tem.pdf
- Safety Behaviours, Human Factors – Resource Guide for Pilots, CASA 2009
- Human Factors for the Private and Commercial Pilot Licences, Aviation Theory Centre 2017
- Performance Levels and Main Error and Violation Types (adapted from Rasmussen and Reason) Airbus Flight Ops Briefing Notes, 2005
- Merritt A. & Klinect J., (2006). Defensive Flying for Pilots: An Introduction to TEM
- Doc 9859 Safety Management Manual, ICAO, Montreal
- Threat And Error Management (TEM), Captain Dan Maurino, Coordinator, Flight safety and Human Factors Programme – ICAO, Canadian Aviation Safety Seminar (CASS),Vancouver, BC, 18 -20 April 2005.
- http://wikiofscience.wikidot.com/quasiscience:aeronautical-decision-making
- https://www.faa.gov/regulations_policies/handbooks_manuals/aviation/risk_management_handbook/media/rmh_ch05.pdf
- http://www.pilotfriend.com/training/flight_training/human/decisions.htm
- http://www.free-online-private-pilot-ground-school.com/Aeronautical_decision_making.html
- CAAP 215-1(2): Guide to the preparation of Operations Manuals https://www.casa.gov.au/sites/g/files/net351/f/_assets/main/download/caaps/ops/215-1-annexb.pdf
- Transport Canada – Multi-Crew Operations http://www.tc.gc.ca/eng/civilaviation/standards/commerce-manuals-multicrewsop-menu-1796.htm
- Skybrary, http://www.skybrary.aero/index.php/Normal_Checklists_and_Crew_Coordination_(OGHFA_BN), Normal Checklists and Crew Coordination